SO YOU THINK YOU KNOW

MAN UTD?

Hodder Children's Books

a division of Hodder Headline Limited

J 796·334

Published in Great Britain in 2006
by Hodder Children's Books

Editor: Isabel Thurston
Design by Fiona Webb
Cover design: Hodder Children's Books

1

ISBN-10: 0340 91720 2
ISBN-13: 9780340917206

Printed by Bookmarque Ltd, Croydon, Surrey

The paper and board used in this paperback by
Hodder Children's Books are natural recyclable products
made from wood grown in sustainable forests. The
manufacturing processes conform to the environmental
regulations of the country of origin.

Hodder Children's Books
a division of Hodder Headline Limited
338 Euston Road
London NW1 3BH

CONTENTS

INTRODUCTION

So you think you know everything about
Manchester United? Reckon you can recall all
the great players, games and achievements of
one of the world's most famous football clubs?
Then this is definitely the book for you!
Contained within its covers are over 1000
questions about the club from its earliest
beginnings right up to United's first game of
2006 versus Arsenal. The questions are graded
into easy, medium and hard. Work your way
through, and look out for those hard grade
questions – some are as tricky as a run by
Ronaldo or as difficult as stopping Ruud or
Rooney scoring. We hope you enjoy the book.

About the author

Clive Gifford is an award-winning author of
over eighty books including *The Kingfisher
Football Encyclopedia*, *Football Skills* and
Fantastic Football. He is the author of Hodder
Children's Books' *So You Think You Know*
series of quiz books including titles on the
English Premier League, David Beckham and
The World Cup. Clive lives in Manchester
and can be contacted at his website:
www.clivegifford.co.uk.

EASY QUESTIONS

1. At which ground does Manchester United play?

2. What is the main colour of Manchester United's home shirt?

3. Which of Manchester United's fierce rivals plays at Stamford Bridge?

4. In which position does Edwin van der Sar play?

5. Who was the manager of the club at the start of the 2005/06 season?

6. Did United legend Bryan Robson play in defence, midfield or attack?

7. If United were playing a Premier League game at the Stadium of Light, would they be playing Newcastle, Sunderland or Middlesbrough?

8 In what year did Phil Neville leave Manchester United?

9 Manchester United let in the Premier League's first ever goal: true or false?

10 Is Manchester United's nickname 'The Red Devils', 'The Irons' or 'The Superhoops'?

11 Who won the 2004/05 Premier League?

12 Who, whilst playing for United, was the first ever Frenchman to score in an FA Cup Final?

13 Did United win the Treble in 1996/97, 1998/99 or 2000/01?

14 Who cost United more to buy: Jaap Stam, Andy Cole or Fabien Barthez?

15 Who became the most expensive teenager ever in the Premier League in 2004?

16 For which country does Ruud van Nistelrooy play international football?

17 Which brothers won FA Cup Winners' medals in 1996 and 1999?

18 Which rivals of United went unbeaten throughout the 2003/04 Premier League season?

19 Manchester United won the first five FA Youth Cups: true or false?

20 Was Roy Keane, Rio Ferdinand or Gary Neville appointed club captain for the 2005/06 season?

21 When United play a Serie A team in the Champions League, what country is that side from?

22 Which team has won the Premier League more times than any other?

23 Which of Manchester United's fierce rivals plays at Anfield?

24 Of all the Manchester derby matches played, who has won more, United or City?

25 For what country did Roy Keane play international football?

26 Who is the longest serving manager for the same Premier League club?

27 For what country did Fabien Barthez play football?

28 Have Manchester United, Arsenal or Liverpool won the FA Cup the most times?

29 To what team did Manchester United lose the 2005 FA Cup Final on penalties?

30 Which of the Greenhoff brothers scored the most goals for United: Jimmy or Brian?

31 In which decade did the Munich Air Disaster occur: the 1950s, the 1960s or the 1970s?

32 The United home strip features what colour socks?

33 How many times have United won the European Super Cup: once, twice or three times?

34 Cristiano Ronaldo is related to Brazil's Ronaldo: true or false?

35 When United play a Bundesliga side in the Champions League, what country is that team from?

36 What nationality is goalkeeper, Tim Howard?

37 For what country did Ronny Johnsen play: Norway, Sweden or Denmark?

38 Which of United's rivals won the 2004/05 Champions League beating AC Milan?

39 Rio Ferdinand and Les Ferdinand are cousins: true or false?

40 Which current Manchester United player was Best Man at David Beckham's wedding?

41 Which club did Roy Keane join after leaving Manchester United?

42 The United home strip features what colour shorts?

43 Which United footballer played for South Africa in the 1998 and 2002 World Cups?

44 Did Manchester United, Leeds United or Arsenal win the very first Premier League?

45 Which famous United legend played in 79 FA Cup games: George Best or Bobby Charlton?

46 If United were playing at Craven Cottage which Premier League side would they be facing?

47 Which Manchester United and England defender failed to perform a drugs test in 2003?

48 Before Phil left, which of the two Neville brothers had scored more goals for Manchester United: Gary or Phil?

49 For which country does Louis Saha play international football: France, Ghana, or the Ivory Coast?

50 What was the score in the 2005/06 FA Cup replay between United and Burton Albion?

MEDIUM QUESTIONS

1. Which central defender scored an incredible nineteen goals in the 1990/91 season?

2. Which one of the following was not a member of the 1982 Youth Cup Final appearing side: Mark Hughes, Clayton Blackmore, Norman Whiteside, Gary Pallister?

3. What was the first trophy that Roy Keane lifted as captain of Manchester United?

4. Who played for United in the early 1980s and then went on to win the 1988 European Championships with Holland?

5. In 1965, who became the first ever United player to be substituted?

6. Which United legend spent a period on loan with Sheffield Wednesday in 1992?

7   Alex Ferguson only signed one player in the 1990 close season. Was it Roy Keane, Steve Bruce or Denis Irwin?

8   Which Manchester United star played for England Schoolboys before becoming a full international with Wales?

9   Which young United starlet was on loan at Sheffield United in 2005?

10 Manchester United didn't play the rest of their season's fixtures after the Munich Air Disaster: true or false?

11 In the 2003/04 season Louis Saha scored twenty goals. How many were for Fulham: one, three or five?

12 Thomas Heaton is part of United's 2005/06 squad. Is he a goalkeeper, mid-fielder or striker?

13 At which club's ground did David Beckham make his last appearance for Manchester United?

14 Who was the first Brazilian to play for Manchester United?

15 Which defender's autobiography, called *Head to Head*, angered Sir Alex Ferguson, who sold the player to Lazio?

16 In the 1983 Charity Shield versus Liverpool, were United wearing red, blue and yellow, grey or white shirts?

17 What was the name of the bestselling book by Manchester City fan, Colin Shindler?

18 Can you name either of the English clubs Ronny Johnsen played for after leaving United?

19 Which former United player became manager of Coventry, Southampton and Celtic?

20 How many Manchester United players have managed Preston North End?

21 At which sport did Kevin Moran excel for the Pegasus club before joining Manchester United?

22 Who was manager of United when they won the 1977 FA Cup, beating Liverpool?

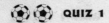

23 Did Gary Neville, Rio Ferdinand or Wayne Rooney score United's second Premier League goal of the 2005/06 season?

24 Which ex-United striker joined Brian Kidd as his assistant at Blackburn Rovers?

25 Which United player made a staggering 246 crosses in the 2003/04 Premier League season?

26 Manchester United manager Frank O'Farrell had been team captain of which London club?

27 Who was captain of the Busby Babes side of the 1950s?

28 Was Tommy Taylor, Bobby Charlton or Jack Rowley signed for an exact figure of £29,999 by Sir Matt Busby?

29 Which United striker was the 2001 PFA Player of the Year?

30 In which season were United offered entry into the European Cup where they were drawn against Young Boys of Berne, only to be refused by the Football Association?

31 United broke the British transfer record for a goalkeeper in 1966 with the purchase of Alex Stepney for: £60,000, £115,000 or £180,000?

32 Which United legend played for all of the following clubs: San Jose Earthquakes, Hibernian, Brisbane Lions and AFC Bournemouth?

33 From which French club did United buy Fabien Barthez: Monaco, Metz or Montpellier?

34 Which manager signed Ray Wilkins: Dave Sexton, Tommy Docherty or Ron Atkinson?

35 Which former United defender became manager of Swedish club, Lyn, in 2005?

36 Who is the most successful player ever at Manchester United, having won sixteen competition medals up to the end of the 2004/05 season?

37 At what German airport did a plane crash occur which killed many of the Busby Babes in 1958?

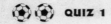

38 Who was Manchester United's second leading scorer in the 2002/03 season: Paul Scholes, David Beckham or Ryan Giggs?

39 Who scored the winning goal in the 1990 FA Cup Final?

40 How much did Alex Ferguson pay for Steve Bruce: nothing, £225,000, £450,000 or £800,000?

41 Who is the most expensive goalkeeper United have ever bought: Taibi, Howard, van der Sar or Barthez?

42 United's 1999 FA Cup squad recorded the song *Lift It High (All About Belief)*. Did they make it to number 24, 11, 8 or 2 in the charts?

43 In the 2003/04 season, did United's reserve team finish third, seventh or eleventh in the FA Premier Reserve League (North)?

44 Which United regular, an attacking midfielder, was suspended for the 1998/99 Champions League Final?

45 Which Third Division team, beginning with the letter W, knocked United out of the FA Cup in 1974/75?

46 Which former Arsenal midfielder claimed in Autumn 2005 that he would never move to Manchester United whilst Ruud van Nistelrooy was there?

47 Which lower division team beat United in the final of the 1991 League Cup?

48 Stan Crowther is famous as the only player to be allowed to play for two different teams in an FA Cup campaign. He was transferred to United shortly after the Munich Air Disaster, but from what Midlands side?

49 In the 1999/2000 season, who did Manchester United thrash 7-1?

50 Was Paul Scholes's one hat-trick for England against Croatia, Poland, Bulgaria or Moldova?

1. Which one of the following was not in the 1992 Manchester United youth team: Nicky Butt, Gary Neville, Roy Keane?

2. In the 2001/02 season, Manchester United's first defeat at home by three or more goals since 1992 occurred. Who won the game?

3. In the 2005/06 season which sports clothing company provided the kit for United: Umbro, Nike, Adidas or Reebok?

4. Was 1934, 1949, 1956 or 1967 the only year that Manchester United have met Manchester City in the Charity Shield?

5. Which newspaper and media owner's attempt to take over the club in 1999 was stopped by the British government?

6. Old Trafford football ground has a nickname including the word 'theatre'. Can you name it?

7. United have played Le Championnat sides in the Champions League. Which country are those sides from?

8 Who made most Premier League appearances for Manchester United in the 2002/2003 season: Mikael Silvestre, Ryan Giggs or Paul Scholes?

9 For a period, Charity Shields were held jointly if the game ended in a draw. How many times have United shared the shield: one, two, three or four?

10 In which decade did Manchester United first win the European Cup: the 1950s, 1960s or 1970s?

11 Who was appointed manager of Scotland for the 1958 World Cup but was unable to manage the side at the tournament?

12 Which famous United player was only the fifth from the club to be capped by Scotland?

13 Who was the longest-serving captain of Manchester United?

14 In United's 1995 9-0 win, who was the only player besides Andy Cole to score more than one goal?

15 Which goalkeeper is the only player to have ever won three sets of League and Cup double winners' medals?

16 Archibald Leitch is remembered as being: the architect of Old Trafford, United's first manager or United's first £100,000 player?

17 With which Premier League club did Andy Cole begin his career: Arsenal, Manchester United or Newcastle United?

18 Which lower league club did United draw in their first game in the 2005/06 Carling Cup?

19 Did Manchester United win, lose or draw their first game after Roy Keane left the club?

20 What was the first club Steve Bruce managed?

21 Danish youngster, Mads Timm made his debut for United in 2002 against: Barcelona, Maccabi Haifa or Partizan Belgrade?

22 Which Argentinian midfielder moved from Manchester United to Chelsea in 2003 for an estimated £17 million?

23 In which season did United win the League and the FA Cup, and get to the final of the League Cup?

24 Was Gary Pallister, Paul Ince or Frank Stapleton voted man of the match in the 1990 Charity Shield?

25 Which club was Arsène Wenger managing the first time a side of his defeated Manchester United?

26 Manchester City's Mike Summerbee co-owned clothes boutiques with which United legend?

27 Can you name one of the three other 'Uniteds' that Peter Beardsley has played for apart from Manchester United?

28 Which Premier League team stunned United with a 4-1 win in October 2005?

29 Which goalkeeper became Manchester United's oldest player since 1921 when he came on as a substitute in the last Premier League game of the 2001/02 season?

30 Was United's 56th unbeaten game at home in European competition against Galatasaray, Rapid Vienna or Brondby?

31 Which two of the following teams beat United at the 2000 FIFA World Club Championship: Vasco da Gama, Real Madrid, Al Nassr, Nexaca, Corinthians?

32 Which striker failed a trial with United at the age of fifteen but later joined the club for a transfer fee of £900,000?

33 Who was the only member of the 1966 United team which played Partizan Belgrade that was not married at the time?

34 Which keeper played just one game for Chelsea before moving to United in 1966?

35 In 1993, was Willie Morgan, Stewart Houston or Mickey Thomas convicted of handling fake bank notes?

36 Peter Schmeichel played in every league
    game of the 1998/99 season: true or
    false?

37 Who, in the 1960s, became the youngest
    ever European Footballer of the Year at
    22 years old?

38 Did Fenerbahce, Inter Milan, Juventus
    or Real Madrid end United's 56 game
    winning streak at home in European
    competitions?

39 Which United manager nearly played for
    the club but his team at the time asked
    for a fee of £150, which put United off?

40 In 2003, which world-famous player was
    the first to score a hat-trick at Old Trafford
    since 1992?

41 From what country are Manchester
    United's old rivals, Benfica?

42 Which Midlands side beat United 3-1 in
    the final of the 1993/94 League Cup?

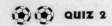

43 What was the name of the club that was
    the forerunner of Manchester United?

44 United manager Jack Rowley also
    managed a famous Dutch club. Can
    you name it?

45 Who was bought first, Wayne Rooney,
    Cristiano Ronaldo or Rio Ferdinand?

46 Who scored more goals for United: Joe
    Spence, Mark Hughes or David Herd?

47 Who was the first United player to play
    in three World Cup Finals?

48 Which former Manchester United
    midfielder was the oldest player to
    represent QPR in the Premier League?

49 Who was United's first million pound
    signing: Gary Birtles, Roy Keane or Bryan
    Robson?

50 Is Fred The Red, The Little Red Devil or
    Busby the official mascot of Manchester
    United?

1. Which United player scored the goal that resulted in Chelsea's first loss in the 2005/06 Premier League?

2. In January 2006, United paid £7 million for Nemanja Vidic but from which club did he come?

3. Was Stuart Pearson, Jimmy Greenhoff or Pat Crerand nicknamed 'Pancho'?

4. In what European competition did United record their record victory of 10-0?

5. In which country was Raimond van der Gouw born?

6. Whose autobiography was entitled *The Good, the Bad and the Bubbly*?

7. How many games did Stewart Houston play for Scotland: one, three, seven or nine?

8. Which team holds the highest average attendance record for every Premier League season?

21

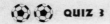

9 Who only appeared 34 times for United in four years at the club before leaving in 2000?

10 Who managed United from 1977 to 1981: Tommy Docherty, Frank O'Farrell or Dave Sexton?

11 Who beat Manchester United 2-0 to win the 2000 Charity Shield?

12 Rutgerus Johannes Martinus are the first names of which United player: Jaap Stam, Kleberson or Ruud van Nistelrooy?

13 Which TV pundit did United player Noel Cantwell replace as manager of Coventry City in 1967?

14 Against whom did Wayne Rooney score his first United hat-trick: Fenerbahce, Bolton Wanderers, Porto or Charlton Athletic?

15 Manchester United scored an amazing 143 goals in one league season. Was it 1956/57, 1967/68 or 1998/99?

16 Against which Merseyside club did United set a record attendance of 72,077 for an English league midweek game, in 1957?

17 Which United player gave away a penalty as England failed to qualify in November 2005 for the U21 Championships?

18 In 1983 did the United team song *Glory, Glory Man United* reach number 13, number 4 or number 1 in the charts?

19 Ole Gunnar Solskjaer scored how many goals against Nottingham Forest in the last twelve minutes of a 1998/99 season game?

20 In 1990, Manchester United drew the FA Cup Final 3-3 with which club?

21 When Manchester United played Arsenal in December 2002, United had just four shots on target. Did any go in?

22 Which club did Nicky Butt join after leaving Manchester United?

23 Who scored the goal that won the 1998/99 Champions League: Dwight Yorke, Teddy Sheringham or Ole Gunnar Solskjaer?

24 David Beckham left Manchester United having made 294, 354, 394 or 454 appearances for the club?

25 Who was the first team to score a goal against Manchester United in the 2004/05 FA Cup: Exeter, Southampton or Newcastle United?

26 Who kept goal for the United States during the 2002 World Cup: Kasey Keller, Tim Howard or Brad Friedel?

27 What country did Mark Hughes manage before returning to club management?

28 On the day that United recorded their biggest ever Premier League win (9-0) David Beckham also scored, but for which club?

29 Was Newton Heath football club made up of bricklayers, railway workers or coal miners?

30   Manchester United's Youth team last won
      the FA Youth Cup in: 1992, 1996 or 2003?

31   At what club was Carlos Queiroz assistant
      manager before being made Real Madrid
      manager?

32   In 80 seasons in England's top division,
      in which position have United most often
      finished?

33   How many players costing over £20
      million have United bought?

34   Did Shay Brennan, Bobby Charlton or
      Bill Foulkes score the first goal for United
      after the Munich Air Disaster?

35   In November 2002, Newcastle United
      scored three goals against United. How
      many did United score in return?

36   Which striker scored on his away debut
      and then broke his leg on his home debut
      for United in 1992?

37   Who saved two penalties from Arsenal
      on his debut in 2003?

38　Referee Mike Riley awarded how many penalties for Manchester United in four League and Cup games at Old Trafford in 2002/03?

39　Did Chris Turner, Gary Bailey or Gary Walsh keep goal for United during the 1991 European Cup-Winners' Cup semi-final?

40　Did former United striker Dion Dublin score his 50th, 100th or 200th goal in all league and cup games in December, 2002?

41　Which United signing from West Ham went on to captain England twice in the 1990s?

42　For which Scottish team did Andrei Kanchelskis play later on in his career?

43　Was Charlie Roberts, Alf Schofield or George Perrins the first United player to be capped for England?

44　Which striker plays for United in the Number 20 shirt?

45 For which country did Paul McGrath play international football?

46 Which Championship side did Manchester United beat to win the 2004 FA Cup?

47 Who scored a hat-trick in the European Cup in 1968, the last scored by United until the late 1990s?

48 Which north-western club recorded United's first Premier League defeat of the 2005/06 season?

49 Which Manchester United player won Match of the Day's Goal Of The Season award for his amazing run and shot against Arsenal in 1999?

50 Which former James Bond star was offered a trial with United in the 1950s?

1. Which Premier League side did United play in their first game after Roy Keane left the club?

2. Which youngster made his debut for England after only playing eleven games for Manchester United?

3. Who replaced Gordon Hill as substitute in both the 1976 and 1977 FA Cup Finals?

4. Who was the only player in the 2005/06 squad with a bird-like name?

5. Which former United keeper won the World Goalkeeper of the Year award in 2000?

6. Who was the first player after Solskjaer to score on his Manchester United debut?

7. Which Premier League player became the youngest England international when he debuted against Australia in 2003?

8. In the first season that United won the Premier League, which team won both the League and FA Cups?

9 Which United goalkeeper came up for an attack against Rotor Volvograd in a European cup tie and scored?

10 Which United player, whilst at another club, helped end Arsenal's 30-game unbeaten streak in November 2002?

11 The official magazine of the club is called: *Old Trafford, The Red Devils* or *United*?

12 How many of the Scottish team that lost to England 5-1 in 1975 were United players at the time?

13 United beat a team from which country to win the 1999 Intercontinental Cup?

14 In 2000, United managed to win a record number of league games in a row. How many games?

15 Which ex-United striker was earlier signed by Aston Villa from Signal Hill in 1989?

16 Which United player was known as 'Captain Marvel': Gordon Strachan, Bobby Charlton or Bryan Robson?

17 Which United midfielder moved to Besiktas in August 2005?

18 All the following players have played for Manchester United and which other side: Lee Sharpe, Gordon McQueen, Rio Ferdinand and Brian Greenhoff?

19 Manchester United bought a striker for over £12 million and sold him a few seasons later to Blackburn Rovers for around £2 million. Who was he?

20 Which former United player with the first names José Pereira was part of a FIFA World Cup-winning team?

21 Did Bobby Charlton, Joe Jordan or Denis Law score a record 27 goals for United in Manchester derby games?

22 In 1960, United beat a Ukrainian National XI. Was the score 4-0, 7-2 or 10-1?

23 Which former United player's cousin is World Championship-winning boxer, Nigel Benn?

24 United started the 2003/04 season with a 4-0 thrashing of which other north-west England side?

25 Which United midfielder was just eighteen when he was made captain of Chelsea?

26 In 1982, United's Youth team lost the FA Youth Cup Final to which team: Crystal Palace, Luton Town, Watford or Liverpool?

27 Old Trafford hosted the Final of the Champions League in: 2003, 2004 or 2005?

28 In Alex Ferguson's first 1000 games in charge, did the team draw more games than they lost?

29 United played Club America on their US tour in 2003: from which country are Club America?

30 Which current United player scored the club's 1000th Premier League goal in October 2005?

31 Which United player was criticized in 2005 for mocking the relegation plight of Southampton?

32 What was the first trophy Alex Ferguson won with Manchester United?

33 Was the name of the company, run by racehorse owners John Magnier and JP McManus, that once owned 29% of Manchester United shares: Magniers, Coolmore or Gibrock?

34 Which former Manchester United footballer was sold to Leeds United for £4.5 million in 1996: Paul Ince, Andrei Kanchelskis or Lee Sharpe?

35 What rank did Sir Matt Busby have in World War II: Corporal, Colonel, Sergeant Major or Private?

36 What was the name of the United player who was the first footballer from any club to be sent off in an FA Cup Final?

37 Which current player has played over 650 games for the club?

38 Which captain of United played 29 times for The Republic of Ireland and nine times for Northern Ireland?

39 Lopez Ricardo was a Manchester United squad player in 2002/03 but was he a goalkeeper, a striker or a midfielder?

40 Which Everton legend scored five goals against United in 1927?

41 Against which team in 1996 did David Beckham score a stunning goal from over 50 metres away?

42 How many matches did Manchester United play in the 2004/05 FA Cup?

43 Which current Manchester United player holds the record for the most goals in a European game for Leeds United, a record he achieved in 2002?

44 Which current United player was named after a former US President?

45 Which ex-United striker released an R'n'B single called *Outstanding* in 2000?

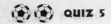

46 In 1965, Manchester United won the league title on goal difference from which club?

47 Which United player was the youngest ever footballer to play in the First Division when he made his debut in 1953?

48 Is Manchester United's new training ground at Carrington, Davyhulme, Stretford or Chester?

49 Was Manchester United's first game of the 2005/06 season against Everton, Debrecen or Wigan Athletic?

50 Who scored all four goals in a game for Manchester United in the 2004/05 season?

1 What is the name of the team formed by supporters opposed to the takeover of Manchester United by Malcolm Glazer?

2 Which Premier League side's old ground was called Roker Park?

3 In October 1985 United opened a ten point gap over their league rivals, but in which position did they finish the season?

4 Did Alan Gowling, Bobby Charlton or Frank Stapleton play in the 1968 British Olympic football team?

5 As of the 2005/2006 season, four of the current United squad had scored more than 100 goals for the club. Can you name two of them?

6 Which former United goalkeeper has a degree in physics from Witts University?

7 Who is the second longest serving manager in the Premier League, after Sir Alex Ferguson?

8 Who sensationally beat Manchester United 6-3 during the 1996/97 season?

9 Fratton Park is the home ground of which Premier League team?

10 Can you name the club Steve Bruce played for straight after leaving Manchester United?

11 Did United beat Estudiantes, Boca Juniors, Palmeiras or Santos 1-0 in the 1999 Intercontinental Cup?

12 In the 1948 FA Cup campaign, United played none of their games at Old Trafford. Can you name any one of the three other club's grounds used for United's home ties?

13 Did Denis Law score 18, 30 or 42 goals for Scotland?

14 Was Manchester United's only victory in the 2000 FIFA World Club Championship against South Melbourne, Corinthians or Nexaca?

15 Which of the Greenhoff brothers was a midfielder turned defender: Jimmy or Brian?

16 Which trophy did Tommy Docherty win in his last game as manager of United?

17 Which United player scored a goal for the Rest of the World when they played England in a 1963 match?

18 What football competition final was staged at Old Trafford in 1970?

19 First and second place in the 1968 European Footballer of the Year award both went to United players. Can you name them in order?

20 Which was the one United player to miss a penalty in the shoot-out at the end of the 2005 FA Cup Final?

21 Which Manchester United player is known as the 'baby-faced assassin'?

22 Which former United favourite is the youngest player ever to appear at a World Cup?

23 Christies sold a pair of which player's boots from the 1997/98 season at auction for £13,800?

24 For the 2005/06 season, who wore the Number 2 shirt?

25 Manchester United won their first match of the 1967/68 European Cup 4-0 against which Scottish team: Rangers, Hibs, Dundee or Hearts?

26 Which player joined in 2003, made his debut against Bolton Wanderers and by the autumn of 2005 had made over 100 appearances for United?

27 In the 2005/06 season, did Alan Smith, Wayne Rooney or Liam Miller play in the Number 14 shirt?

28 Who made three penalty saves for United in a single game versus Ipswich in 1980?

29 Was United's former training ground called The Parks, The Cliff, The Ledge or The Slopes?

30 Did Ruud van Nistelrooy score four goals in a game against Sparta Prague, Portsmouth or Fulham in the 2004/05 season?

31 Which United legend is accredited with first calling Old Trafford, 'the Theatre of Dreams'?

32 Which former United manager had a book published about him in 1998, called *A Different Ball Game*?

33 Who did Manchester United play in the Final when they first won the European Cup?

34 Which United player co-holds the Premier League record for the most goals scored in a game?

35 How many times have Manchester United paid out a British record fee for a goalkeeper?

36 When United play a La Liga team in the Champions League, what country is that team from?

37 Did United beat Coleraine, Limerick or Shamrock Rovers 6-0 in the European Cup-Winners' Cup in 1964?

38 Who did Manchester United beat in the quarter-final of the 2003/04 FA Cup?

39 QPR's Dennis Bailey scored a hat-trick at Old Trafford against United in 1992. In what year did this next happen?

40 Who was the first Manchester club to win the FA Cup: United or City?

41 Which former United striker was manager of the team that consigned United to their first Premier League defeat of the 2005/06 season?

42 When Paul Ince left United, which Italian club did he move to?

43 Was the sponsor on the 2005/06 shirts a drinks, mobile phone or computer company?

44 When the Premier League began in 1992, who was manager of United's arch-rivals, Liverpool?

45 What number shirt did Rio Ferdinand have for the 2005/06 season?

46 Which United legend has a statue in his honour in the upper concourse of the Stretford End, unveiled in 2002: George Best, Bryan Robson or Denis Law?

47 From what Scottish club was Liam Miller signed by United?

48 Which ex-United midfielder is in a coaching role with the first team at Manchester United?

49 Who managed United from 1972 to 1977: Tommy Docherty, Ron Atkinson or Dave Sexton?

50 Where did Manchester United finish in the 2001/02 season?

QUIZ 6

1 The biggest 2002/03 Premier League crowd of the season saw United play which London team?

2 How old was George Best when he died?

3 Who was the second United player to play for England in three World Cup Finals?

4 What sport would you watch at the other Old Trafford ground in Manchester?

5 Which player scored two goals on his Old Trafford debut in 1993?

6 What colour shirts did United wear in the 1968 European Cup Final?

7 Which United player held the record as the youngest ever England international from 1955 until Michael Owen debuted in 1998?

8 What country is Quinton Fortune from?

9 Who returned from suspension to score an astonishing six goals in United's 8-2 thrashing of Northampton Town in the 1970 FA Cup?

10 Did former United striker Dion Dublin score his 100th Premier League goal in 1998, 2002 or 2004?

11 Between December 1975 and February 1976, United played how many games in a row with an unchanged starting eleven?

12 Which team won the 1998 Charity Shield, beating Manchester United 3-0?

13 Who was the club's manager immediately before Sir Alex Ferguson?

14 Were Chelsea, Liverpool, Manchester United or Arsenal the first club in England to have their own dedicated TV channel?

15 Which one of the following players did not appear for United before his 17th birthday: Duncan Edwards, Sammy McIlroy, Steve Bruce, Norman Whiteside?

16 Which rival side's old ground used to be Maine Road?

17 Against which north-west of England side did Darren Ferguson play his last Premier League game?

18 At which club was Andy Cole when he scored 34 goals in a single Premier League season?

19 At the end of the 2000/01 Premier League season, how many points did Manchester United finish ahead of the runners-up?

20 In 1938, United goalkeeper Tommy Breen touched a throw-in but didn't stop it, resulting in a goal scored from a throw-in: true or false?

21 From which club did Alex Ferguson sign Steve Bruce?

22 Which United player remains England's leading international goal scorer?

23 Enoch 'Knocker' West played 192 times for Manchester United. Did he score 3, 27, 49 or 82 goals?

24 Can you name any one of the four Italian teams that played in the Anglo-Italian Cup in 1973?

25 Sir Alex Ferguson's middle name is the same as the surname of United's manager between 1921 and 1926. What is the name?

26 Was Remi Moses, Laurie Cunningham or Dennis Walker the first black player to play for Manchester United?

27 Which tough defender joined United for a bargain £30,000 in 1983?

28 In 2003, Manchester United went on a US tour and played four friendly games. How many did they win?

29 Did United sign Edwin van der Sar from PSV Eindhoven, Royal Antwerp or Fulham?

30 In the 2003/04 Champions League, Manchester United scored five goals against Panathinaikos, but from which country does that club come?

31 In the 1999/2000 season, did United suffer three, five, seven or nine league defeats?

32 In the 1963/64 season, which player had an amazing strike rate of 30 goals in 30 appearances?

33 Which one game of Euro 96 did Gary Neville miss out due to suspension?

34 After drawing the first game of the 1990 FA Cup Final, did United win, draw or lose the replay?

35 Which player's only hat-trick in the thirteen years he played for United was actually for the England national team in 1984?

36 Which United legend helped represent Japan's bid to host the World Cup?

37 Who beat United in the 1958 FA Cup Final: Bolton Wanderers, Birmingham City or Blackburn Rovers?

38 Manchester United's first ever game in the Football League was against: Leyton Orient, Accrington Stanley or Gainsborough Trinity?

39 At which World Cup did Roy Keane have a dispute with the manager and leave the World Cup squad?

40 Can you name either of the clubs managed by Ron Atkinson which knocked United out of the League Cup in 1991 and 1994?

41 The three Wallace brothers, Danny, Rod and Ray all played for Southampton, but which one played for Manchester United?

42 Who did Roy Keane take over the captaincy of Manchester United from?

43 Which two brothers won FA Cup winners' medals in 1977?

44 In 1957, what feature did Old Trafford get permanently for the first time?

45 Who beat United 4-1 at Old Trafford on the first day of 1992?

46 Between the 1992/93 and the 2004/05 seasons, against which team have United scored 37 goals in just thirteen Premier League home games?

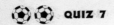

47 What did United go without during 73 games between 1988 and 1990?

48 Which former United manager became coach of Iran's national team?

49 Was Bryan Robson, Gordon Strachan or Peter Schmeichel 37 years and 92 days old when he scored against Oldham in the FA Cup semi-final?

50 Which player, whose real first name is Luigi, scored 97 goals for United between 1972 and 1984?

 QUIZ 7

1 What was the last cup final in which United played in white shirts?

2 Who scored two goals in the 3-1 defeat of Charlton in November 2005?

3 Which United player scored both goals for England in their Euro 2000 first play-off game against Scotland?

4 Which Arsenal player scored the winning goal in the 2003 FA Cup Final?

5 Can you name either of the players who survived the Munich Air Disaster and played in United's first game after it?

6 In 1996, who did United beat in the Charity Shield 4-0?

7 Did Lee Sharpe, Ray Wilkins or Neil Webb become the 1000th England international in 1987?

8 For what country does John O'Shea play international football?

9 How many United players played in England's memorable 3-2 victory over Argentina in November 2005?

10 Which former United legend managed West Bromwich Albion when they escaped relegation at the end of the 2004/05 season?

11 To which of United's rivals did Chief Executive Peter Kenyon move?

12 Which former United striker was the highest scorer in the Spanish league in the 2004/05 season?

13 United broke the club transfer record in 1988 to spend £1.8 million to bring a player back for his second spell at the club. Who was he?

14 Roy Keane joined Manchester United from which club?

15 What is the only team that United have played in the Premier League who now play under a different name?

16 Did Wayne Rooney, David Bellion or Ruud van Nistelrooy score a hat-trick in the 2004/05 season?

17 Which season went right down to the last game, with Manchester City winning the title from Manchester United by two points?

18 Against which London team were United playing in 1994 when Peter Schmeichel was sent off?

19 United have won the league championship how many times: eleven, thirteen or fifteen times?

20 Who did Manchester United beat in the semi-final of the 2003/04 FA Cup?

21 Who won the French Championship with Marseilles in 1991, the English League with Leeds in 1992 and the English League with United in 1993 and 1994?

22 What position did Denis Irwin play?

23 Was Bobby Charlton, Denis Law or Johnny Carey the first United player to win the Football Writers' Footballer of the Year award?

24 In August 2005, Manchester United let two players go on loan to Swindon Town. Can you name either of them?

25 Which ex-United striker did United keeper, Ricardo, bring down to concede a penalty in his first game for the club?

26 Which Welsh winger owns the most Premier League winners' medals of any player?

27 What is former United striker Mark Hughes's real first name?

28 What shirt number did Paul Ince, Gordon Strachan and Jimmy Greenhoff all wear?

29 What part of his body did Ole Gunnar Solskjaer seriously injure in September 2003?

30 Which United keeper only let in 22 goals in 39 games for the club in the 1981/82 season: Jimmy Rimmer, Gary Bailey or Les Sealey?

31 In 2005, Manchester United played two teams whose home grounds are both called St James Park. Can you name them?

32 Manchester United have won seventeen league championships: true or false?

33 For which nation does Ole Gunnar Solskjaer play international football?

34 Against which London team were United playing when Eric Cantona launched his infamous 'kung-fu kick' at a supporter in the crowd?

35 Who was the first player or manager of United to receive a knighthood?

36 Who scored more goals for Manchester United: Brian McClair or Tommy Taylor?

37 Who was in goal for United against Tottenham Hotspur in 2005 when he dropped the ball over his goal line, yet a goal wasn't given?

38 In 1995, who were United's opponents in a replay when a record low attendance for an FA Cup semi-final match (17,987) was recorded?

39 Harry Gregg dragged an unconscious player from the Munich plane crash. The player recovered to play again for United. Who was he?

40 How many games did it take Diego Forlan to score his first Premier League goal: 8, 16 or 24 games?

41 For the 2005/06 season whose squad number is 1: Roy Carroll's, Tim Howard's or Edwin van der Sar's?

42 Did the 100th Manchester derby take place in 1974, 1980, 1987 or 1991?

43 Who, in 1990, became the first ever player to captain a team to win three FA Cups?

44 The highest Premier League attendance in the 2004/05 season was at Old Trafford, but were United playing Chelsea, Arsenal or Portsmouth?

45 How many hat-tricks did United players score in the 2004/05 season?

46 Which former player is in charge of the U19 team at Manchester United?

47 Did United win every game they played in during August 2005?

48 How many England caps did United centre back Steve Bruce gain for England?

49 Who cost United more to buy: Massimo Taibi, Roy Keane or Jesper Blomqvist?

50 Who scored the last goal of Manchester United's 2004/05 Premier League campaign?

QUIZ 8

1 Was Eric Cantona, Brian McClair or Mark Robbins the scorer of the first ever hat-trick in the Premier League?

2 Has Mark Hughes been awarded an OBE, an MBE or both?

3 Who did Manchester United beat in the 2003/04 FA Cup Final?

4 Which defender was at Turkish team, Besiktas, before signing for United and once appeared on the official club photograph sporting a black eye?

5 Who did Manchester United draw with in the third round of the 2005/06 FA Cup?

6 Which United player is the only one to have scored four goals in a single Champions League match?

7 Nikola Jovanovic made 25 appearances for United but did he come from Yugoslavia, the Czech Republic or Estonia?

8 Which Scottish club did United beat 4-0 on their 2003 US tour?

9 Who was manager of the side that knocked United out of the 2003/04 Champions League?

10 Manchester United once went a record 27, 34 or 56 games unbeaten at home in European competitions?

11 Sylvan Ebanks-Blake is a young member of the 2005/06 United squad; from which country does he come?

12 Manchester United, Arsenal and which other Premier League club entered the 2000/01 Champions League?

13 Was United's last game before the start of the 2003/04 season against Juventus, Benfica or Stoke City?

14 Which United player, nicknamed 'Stroller', later became the manager of Arsenal?

15 How many games did two United keepers, Jimmy Rimmer and Alex Stepney each play for England?

16 Who took the penalties for United in the first few months of the 1973/74 season: Denis Law, Bobby Charlton or Alex Stepney?

17 Which former Premier League side played at Oakwell?

18 Newton Heath originally played at which ground: North Road, Bank Street or Maine Road?

19 Did United striker, Louis Saha score 12, 22 or 32 goals in his first season with his previous English club, Fulham?

20 Can you name the four Premier League clubs Teddy Sheringham has played for in the past ten years?

21 Can you recall any of the three clubs Alex Ferguson's son, Darren, played for apart from United?

22 Which United legend's brothers, Gary and Justin, also played professional football in England?

23 Did United lose 11%, 15% or 23% of all the games in which Eric Cantona played?

24 Which player only played five games in the 1992/93 season, but at Steve Bruce's insistence lifted the Premier League trophy along with Bruce?

25 Which of the following players did United spend the most in signing: David Bellion, Tim Howard or Eric Djemba-Djemba?

26 Can you name any one of the three sons of Malcolm Glazer who were appointed to the board that runs the club?

27 United won the 1992-93 league season, but in what place were they in the league after the first two games?

28 In the 1999/2000 season, how many Premier League games did United lose at home: none, one or two?

29 What nationality was Sir Matt Busby: English, Scottish or Irish?

30 Who performed the rare feat of scoring a hat-trick both home and away against the same team, Burnley, in the 1960/61 season: Denis Law, Dennis Viollet or Bill Foulkes?

31 In the summer of which year did Ruud van Nistelrooy join Manchester United?

32 Which midfielder became United's most expensive sale at the time when he left Manchester in 1995 for £7 million?

33 Jimmy Murphy was Sir Matt Busby's long-serving assistant, but which team did he manage at the 1958 World Cup finals?

34 Kevin Keegan's last game for Liverpool was a loss against United in which competition?

35 Did Roy Keane join United in 1993, 1995 or 1997?

36 Is the new museum opened at the ground in 1998 in the North, East or West Stand?

37 In 2004, Welling United's manager was a former United and England World Cup defender. Who was he?

38 Who was the first United player to captain England: Bobby Charlton, Paul Ince or Bryan Robson?

39 To which Premier League club was Kieran Richardson on loan in the 2004/05 season?

40 United's worst ever league defeat was a 7-0 loss against: Blackpool, Bradford City or Blackburn Rovers?

41 Eddie McIlvenny played for a short while for United in the 1950s, but he was better known as captain of which national team that beat England at the 1950 World Cup?

42 Who cost United more to buy: Gabriel Heinze, Tim Howard or Henning Berg?

43 Which current United star scored a hat-trick on his debut for the club?

44 United's first ever game in the European Cup in 1956 was also their highest ever European score, 10-0: true or false?

45 In 1994, Ryan Giggs had what part of his body removed?

46 In the 1998/99 season, what was the name of Alex Ferguson's assistant who left to become a manager in his own right?

47 Who managed United from 1970 to 1971: Frank O'Farrell, Dave Sexton or Sir Matt Busby?

48 Who scored the very first goal of Manchester United's 2005/06 season?

49 Which BBC football commentator was on loan to United in 1983-84?

50 Which football club did legendary United manager, Sir Matt Busby join when he was seventeen years old?

1. How many United players died in the Munich Air Disaster: three, five, eight or twelve?

2. Ruud van Nistelrooy scored his first goal for United in 2001. In which year did he score his 100th?

3. Did Clayton Blackmore, Roy Keane or Mike Duxbury play 381 times for United, scoring seven goals?

4. Which United manager was also manager of the 1948 British Olympic football team?

5. Which former director of the BBC was also once a director of Manchester United?

6. Who scored four goals in just seventeen minutes in a Premiership match which United won 8-1?

7. Dwight Yorke will finally make a World Cup finals appearance after Trinidad and Tobago beat which side in the World Cup qualifying play-offs?

8 Which United striker broke his cheekbone in a March 2006 reserve team game?

9 United won the 1995/96 Premier League title despite their leading scorer only netting seven, ten or fourteen goals?

10 Was Sylvan Ebanks-Blake given the shirt number 27, 40, 51 or 99 when he made his first team debut for Manchester United?

11 How many points did United finish behind Chelsea in the 2004/05 Premier League season: seven, eleven or eighteen?

12 The £500,000 transfer of Tony Coton was the most expensive transfer directly between Manchester United and which other club?

13 From what country are Manchester United's old rivals, PSV Eindhoven?

14 Between 1999 and 2001, did United use more than three, more than five or more than eight different goalkeepers?

 **QUIZ 9**

15 In Alex Ferguson's first 1000 games in charge, did the team score 1203, 1542 or 1784 goals?

16 Tommy Docherty signed a winger for Manchester United and signed him twice more whilst at other clubs. Who was the player?

17 Who signed Paul McGrath for just £30,000 from St Patrick's Athletic?

18 How many goals has Paul Scholes scored for England: 14, 17, 19 or 22?

19 Peter Beardsley played one match for Manchester United before he was released: true or false?

20 The winners of the 1966 and the 1967 Footballer of the Year awards were brothers, one of whom played for United. Can you name them?

21 Which former United player was manager of West Bromwich Albion during the exciting end to the 2004/05 season?

22 Was Mick McCarthy, Jack Charlton or Brian Kerr in charge of his country's team when Roy Keane returned to international football?

23 Who was the last player Sir Matt Busby signed for United: Stuart Pearson, Willie Morgan or Sammy McIlroy?

24 In the early 1980s, who was United's leading goal scorer for three seasons in a row?

25 Which two lesser-known trophies did United win in 1991?

26 The new West Stand, replacing the old Stretford End in 1993 cost: £2.5, £4.8, £7.1 or £10.3 million?

27 Which manager left United after having an affair with the wife of the physiotherapist?

28 Can you name all of United's 2005/06 Premier League rivals whose names end in the word, 'Athletic'?

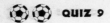

29 Which pair of United players who were also brothers were the subject of the book, *For Club and Country*?

30 Which ex-United player is coach of France's national five-a-side beach soccer team?

31 Did Joe Jordan, Phil Neville or Stuart Pearson score the most goals for United?

32 Which player was signed from Middlesbrough, played from 1989 to 1998, and then left United to return to Middlesbrough?

33 Sandy and Sheena unveiled a monument to their father in 1996: who was their father?

34 Michael Knighton attempted to take over Manchester United. Did he later become chairman of Aston Villa, Crystal Palace or Carlisle United?

35 Which two of the following players have played for both Manchester City and Manchester United: Billy Meredith, Phil Neville, John Gidman, Arthur Albiston?

36 In the 1997/98 season was United's last Premier League game at Oakwell, Old Trafford or Highfield Road?

37 In which year did ex-United striker Mark Hughes formally retire as a player to concentrate on being the manager of the Welsh national team?

38 Which United player scored twice for England as they beat USA 2-1 in 2005?

39 United forward David Herd scored an unusual hat-trick in 1966. Was it unusual because it involved three diving headers, three penalties or because each goal was scored against a different goalkeeper?

40 Which pair of brothers, one a United player, played for England together 28 times?

41 In the FA Cup Final when Kevin Moran was sent off, did United win, lose or lose after a replay?

42 Who did United draw in the fourth round of the 2005/06 Carling Cup?

43 Which ex-United midfielder managed his own son at Coventry City?

44 Which Londoner who would go on to play for United, turned up at a Tottenham Hotspur trial wearing a Manchester United shirt?

45 Did Paul Parker move to United for one, two or three million pounds in 1991?

46 United have won the league championship fifteen times but how many managers have managed them to a championship title?

47 If United were playing a match at the Hawthorns, which team would they be playing against?

48 Did Ryan Giggs, Roy Keane or Bill Foulkes make 679 appearances for Manchester United?

49 Did Roy Keane make his debut for United in the League Cup, the Charity Shield, the Champions League or the FA Cup?

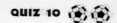
50 What was the first year that the Premier League was won by a team not from the north-west of England?

QUIZ 10

1 Who knocked United out of the 1957 European Cup on their way to winning the trophy?

2 The British transfer fee record was broken by both Manchester United and Manchester City for the same player. Who was he?

3 Which team did Bobby Charlton manage shortly after retiring from playing for United?

4 In the very first Manchester derby game in 1894, United player, Dick Smith, scored four goals: true or false?

5 In the 1999/2000 season, what competition did Manchester United withdraw from, resulting in much criticism?

6   Up to the end of the 2003 season, Norwich's Ruel Fox was the last person to do what at Old Trafford in the Premier League (in 1993)?

7   Which England manager stated that United's Steve Coppell was the first name on his England teamsheet?

8   Which Manchester United legend's mother played hockey for Northern Ireland: Frank Stapleton, George Best or Roy Keane?

9   Which former United defender was a 1998 World Cup winner?

10   Newton Heath's first game in the Football League resulted in a loss to which side, that United now play in the Premier League?

11   Which United forward had an economics degree and scored four goals against Southampton in 1971?

12   Which United player became the first England team member to be sent off on home soil during an international?

13 Did Blackburn Rovers win the 1994/95 Premier League by a one, three, five or nine point margin?

14 What is the name of the American Football club which Malcolm Glazer owns?

15 Eric Cantona won the Football Writers' Association Footballer of the Year in: 1994, 1996 or 1998?

16 Which famous Spanish team did United beat in the final of the European Cup-Winners' Cup in 1991?

17 Did George Best, Denis Law or Bobby Charlton score six goals in a single 1970 FA Cup game?

18 Which England captain wore the Manchester United Number 7 shirt in the 1980s?

19 In 1991, what cup competition were United declared to have won, after the second leg of the two-legged final was not held for political reasons?

20 From which Italian club did United buy Mikael Silvestre?

21 Which former Manchester United player is the Czech Republic's most-capped footballer?

22 In 1997, who scored United's first hat-trick in the European Cup/Champions League since 1968?

23 Which United striker played a match for Stockport County with his father, Alex?

24 Which legend was put on the club's transfer list in 1970 for £60,000?

25 From which club did United sign defender, Paul Parker?

26 How many United players were on the shortlist for the FIFA World Player of the Year 2005 awards?

27 In Alex Ferguson's first 1000 games in charge, did the team lose 190, 244 or 346 matches?

28 What degree did Brian McClair study for but not complete at Glasgow University: sports science, mathematics or sociology?

29 Which Premier League team played at Anfield before Liverpool?

30 In 1961, did Bobby Charlton, Nobby Stiles or Denis Law score an own goal and a regular goal in a game versus Manchester City?

31 From what country does Park Ji-Sung come?

32 Which side were most recently relegated from the English first division: Manchester United, Arsenal or Chelsea?

33 After winning the league in 1967, was the next time United won it in 1972, 1979, 1984 or 1993?

34 Was United's last game on British soil before the Munich Air Disaster held at Highbury, Old Trafford, Anfield or Wembley?

35 In 1950, Charlie Mitten left United to play in which South American country, only to be forced to return to United later when he was suspended for six months?

36 Against which team did Wayne Rooney score his first England goal when no longer a teenager?

37 What is the name of the enormous club shop housed in Old Trafford's East Stand?

38 When United won the league in 1957 who came second: Everton, Wolverhampton Wanderers or Blackpool?

39 Who was the second ever manager to have managed United and the Scotland national team?

40 Who was manager of his national side when Roy Keane left the squad at the 2002 World Cup?

41 Which current United player was the first to receive the PFA Young Player of the Year trophy two years in a row?

42 Which United legend died in November 2005?

43 Which striker in the 1993/94 season scored at Wembley in four different club matches?

44 How many United managers have had two spells in charge of the club?

45 Former United midfielder Eric Djemba-Djemba came from: Nigeria, Cameroon or South Africa?

46 Which United player was the Champions League highest scorer in 2002/03?

47 In 1970/71, David Sadler took over the Number 6 position from which long-serving United player?

48 How old was George Best when he first played for Northern Ireland?

49 Which United striker is Scotland's joint leading scorer, with Kenny Dalglish?

50 In the 1982/83 season who did United beat after an FA Cup Final replay?

1   Which United legend is Denmark's most-capped player?

2   How many times have Manchester City finished above Manchester United in the Premier League: once, twice, three times or never?

3   Was Jesper Blomqvist bought by United from Barcelona, Malmo or Parma?

4   Bob Bishop is remembered as the person who spotted the talents of which two of the following three legends: Norman Whiteside, Roy Keane, George Best?

5   How many games in a row did Peter Schmeichel play for United in the early 1990s: 45, 67, 94 or 128?

6   Were Chelsea, Arsenal or Southampton the first team to beat Manchester United in the 1999/2000 season?

7   Which player, with the first name Norbert, is the proud owner of both a World Cup and European Cup-Winners' medal?

8 Which Irish player has made over 170 appearances for United and went on loan to Bournemouth in 2000?

9 Which United keeper formerly played for South African side, Kaizer Chiefs?

10 A 2-1 defeat to which club saw United exit the 2005/06 Champions League?

11 From which club did Dwight Yorke join United?

12 Who scored the most goals for Manchester United: Stan Pearson, Stuart Pearson or Gary Pallister?

13 Which famous football pundit said, 'You can't win the league with kids' on television in 1995 after a young Manchester United side were well beaten?

14 Who cost Manchester United more: Rio Ferdinand, Wayne Rooney or Louis Saha?

15 How many FA Cups did Manchester United win under Ron Atkinson?

16 If United were playing a match at Upton Park, which team would they be playing against?

17 Billy Meredith was 45 years and 8 months old when he played an international game, but which country did he represent?

18 Which United striker was the 2002 PFA Player of the Year?

19 With which other Premier League side did United tussle to sign Diego Forlan?

20 Which United player joined Brazil's Ronaldinho on the cover of the Playstation 2 FIFA 06 computer game?

21 Which country does former Manchester United striker, Diego Forlan, come from?

22 To the nearest five million, what was Manchester United's income in the 2003/04 season?

23 Which former United midfielder owns a fish and chip shop close to the Old Trafford ground?

24 Did the Premier League begin in 1991, 1992, 1993 or 1994?

25 Which company announced it wanted to buy United for £623 million in 1998?

26 What was Warwick Road North renamed in 1993?

27 Which sponsor of United's announced in November 2005 that it would end its agreement with the club two years earlier than planned?

28 Did Carlos Queiroz, Steve McClaren or Denis Irwin replace Brian Kidd as Alex Ferguson's assistant?

29 Who scored more goals for United: Bryan Robson, Eric Cantona, Teddy Sheringham or Dwight Yorke?

30 Who did United score eleven goals against in their two 2002/03 Premier League games?

31 Which player cost Manchester United the most: Roy Keane, Eric Djemba-Djemba, Peter Schmeichel, Henning Berg?

32   In Autumn 2005, youth and reserve team coach Ricky Sbragia left United to become first team coach of which other north-west England club?

33   Did Bryan Robson gain 45, 62, 71 or 90 caps for England?

34   Who did Manchester United play in their first Premier League game of the 2005/06 season?

35   Which United captain, earlier in his career, was the youngest captain of Aberdeen?

36   Who was voted player of the decade at the 2003 PFA Awards: Roy Keane, Alan Shearer, David Seaman or David Beckham?

37   Which United keeper was the only one to win the World Goalkeeper of the Year award twice?

38   Gerry Daly was signed by United from Bohemians for: £22,000, £115,000 or £240,000?

39 Who did United beat 1-0 in the first leg of the 1991 European Super Cup Final: Red Star Belgrade, Marseilles or Sampdoria?

40 In what place did Manchester United finish in the 2003/04 Premier League?

41 Can you name either of the other English clubs Jesper Blomqvist played for apart from United?

42 Which Premier League manager sold his own son for £250,000 to Wolverhampton Wanderers?

43 Did United beat Everton, Liverpool or Derby County to win the 1985 FA Cup?

44 Which Manchester United midfielder put in a transfer request in January 2004?

45 What was the name of the competition United played in, run to celebrate the crowning of Queen Elizabeth in 1953?

46 Who managed United from 1981 to 1986: Tommy Docherty, Ron Atkinson or Dave Sexton?

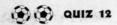

47 Was Jaap Stam signed by United in 1996, 1997, 1998 or 1999?

48 Which Premier League club offered over £20 million for Wayne Rooney but were pipped by Manchester United?

49 Who scored a fabulous lobbed goal at Euro 96 shortly before joining Manchester United?

50 Were United in the first, second or third division in 1974/75?

 QUIZ 12

1 Was Ernest Mangall, Clarence Filditch or John Robson the first United manager to win the league championship?

2 Which former United player is now a postman: Alan Gowling, Jim Leighton or Neil Webb?

3 Which great United player was nicknamed 'El Beatle' in the 1960s?

4   What is the name of the son of a famous United goalkeeper, now on the books at Manchester City?

5   In 2003/04, which player made 34 Premier League appearances, more than any other United team-mate?

6   In the year 1982, United had three different captains. One was Martin Buchan; can you name either of the other two?

7   Which 2005/06 Premier League team play not far from United at the JJB Stadium?

8   Can you name either of the two English teams Denis Irwin played for before joining United?

9   Which United legend became the first ever player to miss a penalty in a shoot-out?

10 Is Bobby Charlton the most, second-most or third-most capped England player of all time?

11 Who was Manchester United's leading goal scorer of 1996/97: Andy Cole, Teddy Sheringham or Ole Gunnar Solskjaer?

12 Did Manchester United, Liverpool or Arsenal become the first team to win the Premier League and FA Cup double?

13 Alan Smith's first goal for England was against Portugal, Poland or Paraguay?

14 Sir Alex Ferguson sold Norman Whiteside to which other English side?

15 How many goals did United let in throughout their whole 2004/05 FA Cup campaign?

16 Manchester United won the FIFA World Club Championship in 2000: true or false?

17 Which Premier League club did Jonathon Spector go on loan to in the 2005/06 season?

18 Was Les Sealey, Peter Schmeichel or Roy Keane nicknamed 'Mr Angry' by his team-mates?

19 At which World Cup was the first goal scored by a United player since 1986?

20 Which player scored on his birthday in the final of the 1968 European Cup?

21 Which United player's wife, Claire, gave birth to his first son, Arron Jake before the 1999/2000 season?

22 Which young striker scored his first Premier League goal on his debut against Sunderland in October 2005?

23 Which defender played a record 62 games for United during the 1993/94 season?

24 Was goalkeeper Paul Rachubka sold to West Ham United, Blackburn Rovers or Charlton Athletic in 2002?

25 In September 2002, did Ryan Giggs, David Beckham or Andy Cole score his 100th goal for Manchester United?

26 At the start of 2004, who was the oldest manager in the Premier League?

27 Was Sammy McIlroy, Lou Macari or Norman Whiteside the youngest player to make his United first team debut since Duncan Edwards?

28 Which former Manchester United legend declared an eleven-year-old David Beckham to be the best player of his age he'd seen?

29 Was Sir Alex Ferguson born in 1938, 1941, 1945 or 1952?

30 What is Manchester United's worst ever finish in the Premier League?

31 At what Scottish club had Alex Ferguson had European success before managing Manchester United?

32 Which ex-United goalkeeper's middle name is Jesse?

33 Which former United player had a tattoo of a native American on his chest?

34 Which team from the north-west of England did United beat 4-1 on New Year's Eve 2005?

35 Which three other Premier League clubs, apart from United, has Peter Schmeichel played for?

36 Who did Manchester United beat to win the 2006 Carling Cup?

37 In which month of 1963 did United have to play four rounds of the FA Cup competition because bad weather had postponed the earlier games?

38 United knocked a team out of the 1990/91 League Cup with a 6-2 win. It was the opposing club's worst defeat at home in 69 years. Who was the team?

39 Which Dutch team played United in Denis Law's testimonial game?

40 Who was awarded the Barclaycard Premiership Player of the Year for 2002/03?

41 For what team was David Bellion playing in the 2005/06 Premier League season?

42 After nine years in charge of Manchester United, Ernest Mangall became manager of which team?

43 Who did United beat 4-0 to win the 1995 FA Cup?

44 In which year was Sir Alex Ferguson in charge of Manchester United for his 1000th match?

45 Which former Manchester United manager said of Dwight Yorke, 'If that lad makes it, my name is Mao Tse-Tung'?

46 Three United players, including Don Givens, all moved together to which team in 1969: Bolton Wanderers, Tranmere Rovers or Luton Town?

47 The highest Premier League attendance in the 2003/04 season was at Old Trafford, but were United playing Southampton, Arsenal or Chelsea?

48 If Gordon Hill played for England, Manchester United had to pay Millwall: £10,000, £100,000 or £1 million?

49 Did 9, 14 or 23 of the 43 passengers on board die in the Munich Air Disaster?

50 Which Manchester United forward cost £12.83 million and scored on his debut versus Southampton?

QUIZ 13

1 Andrei Kanchelskis played for three English teams apart from Manchester United. Can you name two of them?

2 United remained unbeaten at home in European competitions from 1956 until which year?

3 Which team knocked United out of the 2003/04 Champions League: Real Madrid, Porto, Chelsea or Borussia Dortmund?

4 Did Eric Cantona leave United in 1997, 1998, 1999 or 2000?

5 For what country does current United player, Wes Brown, play international football?

6 Was Denis Irwin, Roy Keane or Sammy McIlroy, United's 50th Irish signing?

7 Against whom did United record their record 10-0 victory in a European tie: Anderlecht, Sturm Graz or CSKA Sofia?

8 Who was the first United player to receive the European Footballer of the Year award?

9 Did Inter Milan, Barcelona or Hadjuk Split score six goals against United in a 1980 game?

10 Was Wendy Toms, Karen Brady or Lindsay Cartwright the first female referee's assistant in the Premier League?

11 What were the only two decades of the 20th century in which United didn't win the league or the FA Cup?

12 Who was captain in the first game that United played after Roy Keane left the club?

13 In the 1998/99 Champions League, United shared two epic 3-3 draws in the group stage with which side?

14 What is the name of the café at Old Trafford, the front of which features a brass plaque commemorating United's 1998/99 treble?

15 In the 1911 Charity Shield, United won 8-4, but were their opponents Burnley, Swindon Town or Everton?

16 Who was the first person to score a goal for Manchester United: Harry Stafford, Sandy Turnbull or Chas Richards?

17 What colour was the kit in which United started the match against Southampton in April 1996?

18 Which 'United' finished third behind Manchester United in the 1999/2000 Premier League?

19 How many times has Sir Alex Ferguson been World Soccer's Manager of the Year?

20 In 1991, Manchester United was floated on the London Stock Exchange. Was the club's value approximately £18 million, £98 million, £194 million or £340 million?

21 Including 2005/06, how many different teams have won the Premier League?

22 United have played FA Cup semi-finals at how many different grounds: three, five, seven or ten?

23 With which rival side do United share the record for winning the Charity Shield the most times?

24 What number shirt did Cristiano Ronaldo have for the 2005/06 season?

25 How many defeats did United suffer in their 1968 European Cup campaign?

26 How many FA Cup winners' medals does Ryan Giggs have with United?

27 Who managed United from 1971 to 1972: Frank O'Farrell, Tommy Docherty, Ron Atkinson or Dave Sexton?

28 Les Olive played in goal for United in 1952/53 but his main job was working in the club's ticket office: true or false?

29 In which year during World War II was Old Trafford heavily damaged by German bombing?

30 Were United playing Chelsea, Wigan or Liverpool in 2005 when allegations of the dressing room being bugged first appeared?

31 Who was the only United player to be sent off twice in the 2003/04 season?

32 In 1998/99 which strike partnership yielded an incredible 53 goals that season?

33 Which one of the following players was not a Manchester United player as a teenager: Jonathon Greening, Robbie Savage, Dwight Yorke, Mark Bosnich?

34 Did Aston Villa, Arsenal or Newcastle United finish second to United in the first season of the Premier League?

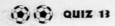

35 Which United player began his career with Cobh Ramblers?

36 Which player scored two goals in United's 8-2 thrashing of Northampton Town in the 1970 FA Cup?

37 Did Lee Sharpe, Gordon McQueen or Arthur Albiston have a spell playing for Grindavik in Iceland?

38 Karel Poborsky left United to join Benfica, Juventus or Lazio?

39 Which United striker who also played for Southampton only won one cap for England?

40 Did Steve Bruce play more than 200, 300 or 400 games for United?

41 Which Italian side did United beat in the semi-final of the 1998/99 Champions League?

42 How many Euro 96 matches were played at Old Trafford?

43 John Sutcliffe played in goal for United in 1903/04 and was also an international in what other sport?

44 Who made his debut, aged eighteen, in the first game of the 2003/04 Premier League season?

45 Does Denis Law, Ruud van Nistelrooy or Andy Cole hold the record for the most goals scored in European competitions?

46 Did United win the FA Youth Cup Final in 1991, 1992 or 1993?

47 Between 1953 and 1957, how many players did Sir Matt Busby buy?

48 Who scored United's winner in the 4-3 win over Real Madrid in 2003?

49 Which famous Northern Ireland and Spurs goalkeeper scored a length of the field goal against United in the 1967 Charity Shield?

50 What nationality is Manchester United defender, Jonathon Spector?

1. Did Peter Davenport, Gary Birtles or Dion Dublin cost United £570,000 in 1985?

2. In the 1998/99 season, Manchester United and which other side suffered just three defeats?

3. For what country did former United goalkeeper, Mark Bosnich play?

4. Young Manchester United players Tom Heaton and Colin Heath were both out on loan in the 2005/06 season at QPR, Swindon Town, Stockport County or Bury?

5. Michael Knighton attempted to take over Manchester United, but in which year?

6. Before his comeback in 2006, Ole Gunnar Solskjaer's last goal for United was in May 2005, October 2004 or September 2003?

7. In March 1980, United lost 6-0 to Liverpool, Newcastle United, Sheffield Wednesday or Ipswich?

8. Was Cristiano Ronaldo signed from Porto, Benfica or Sporting Lisbon?

9 Martin Edwards became Chairman of Manchester United in: 1980, 1984 or 1991?

10 Juan Veron's last game for Manchester United was on the club's 2003 USA tour, but was it against Barcelona, Juventus or Club America?

11 Can you name two of the goalkeepers Manchester United have paid a British record fee for?

12 . What was the name of the famous racehorse that Sir Alex Ferguson and two shareholders in Manchester United, John Magnier and J.P. McManus, fell out over?

13 Which former United player appeared in the Final of the 2004/05 Champions League for AC Milan?

14 When he was a United player, David Beckham was sent out on loan to which other north-west of England club?

15 Who was the leading scorer in the Premier League in the 2002/03 season?

16 In the 2005/06 season, did Gabriel Heinze, Gary Neville or Wes Brown play in the Number 4 shirt?

17 Which two of the following players have played for both Manchester City and Manchester United: Tommy Hutchinson, Brian Kidd, Denis Law, Joe Jordan?

18 In 2003, United won a match 4-3 but were knocked out of the Champions League 6-5 on aggregate. Who were the opposition?

19 Whilst managed by Alex Ferguson, which side became the only Scottish team to win more than one European trophy?

20 How many goals did Peter Schmeichel let in at home throughout the 1994/95 season?

21 Did the Munich Air Disaster occur in 1954, 1958, 1962 or 1964?

22 Who was controversially sold to Chelsea for £1.5 million in 1995: Paul Ince, Mark Hughes or Norman Whiteside?

23 Who was the first English team United ever played in a major European cup competition?

24 What is the official name of Old Trafford's Stretford End?

25 Bobby Charlton was United's top league scorer in 1972/73, with 6, 11, 21 or 28 goals?

26 Can you name either of the United players who played for Denmark at the 1986 World Cup?

27 Between 1992 and 2005, United have led the Premier League in total league points scored. Have they managed over 800, over 900 or over 1000 points?

28 Who scored United's first Premier League goal of the 2005/06 season?

29 In the first Premiership Global Fans Report, which former United player was voted the Premier League's best ever footballer?

30 Were United relegated in 1973/74, 1974/75 or 1975/76?

31 The League Cup was first held in 1961. In what year did United win it for the first time?

32 In August 1941, Manchester United beat New Brighton Tower. How many goals did they score?

33 David Platt was released on a free transfer from Manchester United. Which club did he move to?

34 What is the first name of Gary and Phil Neville's father?

35 Ronnie Wallwork's 1997 debut saw his side beat which Yorkshire team 7-0?

36 Which United player became England's first ever black captain?

37 Which former Manchester United player was in charge of Blackburn Rovers when they were relegated in the 1998/99 season?

38 Who was the only player to be United's leading scorer for five seasons in a row?

39 Who were the only team to beat Manchester United in the 1994/95 Premier League season at Old Trafford?

40 From which club did Manchester United buy Eric Cantona?

41 To which Italian club did United sell Ray Wilkins?

42 Which one of the following goalkeepers scored a penalty against a Ukrainian National XI in 1960: Alex Stepney, Harry Gregg or Alex Dawson?

43 For which country did Karel Poborsky play international football?

44 Did Bill Foulkes play 32, 43 or 61 consecutive FA Cup games for United?

45 Which former United midfielder worked at Walthamstow Greyhound Stadium, has a tattoo of the number seven and has a father-in-law called Tony Adams?

46 Who was just 34 when he became chairman of Manchester United?

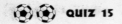
47   In their 2004/05 FA Cup campaign, did Manchester United let in their first goal at the third round, quarter-final or semi-final stage?

48   In the 2004/05 season, was Crystal Palace, Fenerbahce or Exeter City the one team United scored six goals against?

49   Which current defender made his debut for United in 1992 versus Torpedo Moscow?

50   Which current United player held the record for the youngest sportsperson to publish their autobiography in 1994?

 QUIZ 15

1   Who was a miner in St Helens before being picked by Matt Busby, and went on to play eighteen seasons for United?

2   How many players from United were in England's 1970 World Cup squad: none, two, five or nine?

3 Who became the most expensive teenager ever in the Premier League in 2003?

4 Johnny Carey made 344 appearances for United as a full back, winger or goalkeeper?

5 How many games did Gary Neville play in the 2005/06 season before suffering a serious injury?

6 Which United player was the Scottish Footballer of the Year in 1987: Clayton Blackmore, Gordon McQueen or Gordon Strachan?

7 How many times has Sir Alex Ferguson managed United to win the Premier League?

8 In the 2001/02 season which Manchester United winger came on as a substitute against Aston Villa and was then substituted himself later in the game?

9 Which famous Dutch striker was named after United legend, Denis Law?

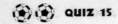

10 Did Steve Bruce hit four, seven, nine or eleven penalties in the 1990/91 season?

11 What was the scoreline in the March 2004 Manchester derby?

12 With which club did Sir Alex Ferguson win the 1977 First Division title in Scotland?

13 Who did Manchester United play in their last 2005/06 Premier League game?

14 United lost their last three Premier League games of which season yet still won the championship?

15 Which competition did United win in 1991 without losing a match on the way?

16 Was Paul Scholes, Jose Antonio Reyes or Cristiano Ronaldo sent off in the 2005 FA Cup Final?

17 Who was the last United player to score a goal in the World Cup before the 1998 tournament?

18 In 1972, who retired for seventeen days before returning to Manchester United?

19 Who became the first United player since Norman Whiteside in 1984 to score a competitive goal on Italian soil?

20 Former United chairman Harold Hardman won a gold medal in football at which Olympics?

21 Was Roy Keane, Gary Pallister or Andrei Kanchelskis the first player ever to be sent off in a League Cup Final?

22 In which Asian country did Gordon McQueen play football after leaving United?

23 Ernie Taylor is one of a handful of players who has appeared in FA Cup Finals for three different clubs. Can you guess two of them?

24 If United were playing at White Hart Lane, which Premier League side would they be playing?

25 Which United player featured when Northern Ireland hosted Portugal for a friendly match in November, 2005?

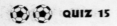

26 How many complete years did Roy Keane spend as a player at Manchester United?

27 Whose last appearance for Manchester United in the Premier League was a 2-0 win against Arsenal in 2002: Paul Ince, David May or Dwight Yorke?

28 In the 2003/04 season, Wolverhampton Wanderers had two ex-United players in their squad. Can you name them?

29 In 1980 which English team missed three penalties against United in an eight minute spell: Birmingham City, Ipswich Town or Southampton?

30 Did George Best, Jack Rowley, Paul Scholes or Andy Ritchie score a hat-trick at age seventeen years and 58 days in just his second game for the club?

31 Who knocked United out of the European Cup at the semi-final stage the year after United had won the competition?

32 Which Manchester United midfielder was signed from Atletico Madrid in 1999?

33 Which Italian side beat United 5-0 shortly after the Munich Air Disaster?

34 Park Ji-Sung was bought from: Perugia, PSV Eindhoven or Porto?

35 Which United manager was once the youngest ever person to referee an FA Cup Final: Ernest Mangall, John Bentley or Herbert Bamlett?

36 Louis Rocca is famous for: buying the club in 1902; suggesting it changed its name to Manchester United; or building Old Trafford?

37 In 1985, which United player became the first to be sent off in a FA Cup Final?

38 Which former Manchester United defender made over 510 appearances for the club from the early 1990s onwards?

39 U4U is the short name of the charity initiative United performs with children around the world. Is this initiative performed with UNICEF, Save The Children, Oxfam or UNESCO?

40 In which month of 2005 did Roy Keane leave Manchester United?

41 Manchester United was a founder member of the football league: true or false?

42 Which United winger played in 206 league games in a row between 1977 and 1981?

43 How many of the teams Manchester United played on their 2003 US tour were from the United States?

44 In 1998/99, which Liverpool player did Dwight Yorke tie with as the Premier League's leading goal-scorer?

45 Which ex-striker was put in charge of Manchester United's academy in 2002?

46 Which United legend was nicknamed 'The King': Denis Law, Mark Hughes or Bobby Charlton?

47 FC United of Manchester played most of their home games in the 2005/06 season at which football club's ground: Blackburn Rovers, Bury or Altrincham?

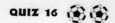

48 Defender Henning Berg has played for which club both before and after his time at Manchester United?

49 Against whom were Manchester United three down at half time in a 2001 Premier League fixture, only to win the match 5-3?

50 Which United manager won two league titles and one FA Cup with the club: Ernest Mangall, John Bentley or Herbert Bamlett?

QUIZ 16

1 Robbie Savage played alongside Gary Neville and David Beckham in the FA Youth Cup winning side: true or false?

2 From 1992/93 to the end of the 2004/05 season, who was the only team to beat United at home four times in the Premier League: Chelsea, Arsenal or Newcastle United?

3 Whose £200,000 move to United in 1973 set a new Scottish transfer record?

4 From what country were Manchester United's 2005/06 Champions League qualifying opponents, Debrecen?

5 In the 1993/94 season, United scored their highest ever total of league points. Was it 85, 88, 90 or 92?

6 Who was the first United player to be sent off in two games in a row?

7 The famous Centre Tunnel is no longer in use, but is it found in the East, West or South Stand at Old Trafford?

8 Which current United player was Wales's youngest ever footballer in a full international?

9 Of the 2005/06 squad, which player has scored the most goals for United?

10 Which club have United legends, Nobby Stiles, Brian Kidd and Sammy McIlroy all managed?

11 Which United player was sent off when the team crashed 6-3 to Southampton in 1996?

12 Which goalkeeper made his debut for United in the 1989/90 season, left the season after and played again for United in 1999/2000?

13 Which England manager between 1946 and 1962 previously played 27 games for Manchester United?

14 Sir Alex Ferguson won the European Cup-Winners' Cup with a team before United. Who was it?

15 Was Sir Alex Ferguson knighted in 1995, 1999 or 2003?

16 Was Tommy Taylor, Jack Rowley or Dennis Viollet nicknamed 'The Smiling Executioner'?

17 Did United sell Dion Dublin to Coventry City, Aston Villa or Middlesbrough for £1,950,000?

18 What colour shirts were United wearing when they suffered four of their six league defeats in the 1995/96 season?

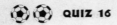

19 Which team has made the most appearances in the Charity Shield: Manchester United, Liverpool or Arsenal?

20 In which country was Diego Forlan playing before he was signed by United?

21 Which player was signed by United in 2003 from MLS team Metrostars?

22 Was United's 1922 signing, Frank Barson, a dentist, blacksmith or vet by trade?

23 Bayern Munich's goal scorer in the Final of the 1998/99 Champions League had the initials M.B. Was it Michael Ballack, Mario Basler or Markus Babbel?

24 Which two of the following grounds did the architect of Old Trafford Stadium also design: Stamford Bridge, Hampden Park, Anfield, White Hart Lane?

25 Which United player scored twice on his England debut in 2005?

26 By how many points did United lose the 1994/95 Premier League title?

27　For what country does current United player Darren Fletcher play international football?

28　Which former United keeper was sacked by Chelsea in 2002?

29　Was 1927, 1957, 1977 or 1997 the last time United played a competitive game on Christmas Day?

30　How much was George Best fined for not training on Christmas Day in 1970: £5, £50, £500 or £5000?

31　Which United legend was bought from Torino in Italy for a then British record of £115,000?

32　Which United player cost £3.75 million in 1993?

33　When Martin Edwards became United's Chairman, he was the second youngest in England. Which pop star was the youngest?

34 Who finished second to United in the Premier League in both the 1995/96 and 1996/97 seasons?

35 In which season did United win the Premier League by an enormous fourteen point margin?

36 Up to the beginning of 2004, only one player, a former United footballer, has ever scored in a Manchester derby, a Merseyside derby and a Glasgow derby. Who is he?

37 What was the score at United's last ever visit to Arsenal's Highbury ground for a league game?

38 Is Sammy McIlroy's middle name, Charlton, Baxter or Busby?

39 Enoch West joined Manchester United in 1910 for a fee of £150, £450 or £2250?

40 What was the name of Real Madrid's manager at the start of the 2003/2004 season?

41 Was the 100th Manchester derby held at Old Trafford, Maine Road or the City of Manchester Stadium?

42 What was the name of Manchester United's only ever Irish manager?

43 Against which rivals did Manchester United lose the Final of the 2003 League Cup?

44 Was Eric Cantona, Andrei Kanchelskis or Mark Hughes United's leading goal scorer in the 1994/95 season?

45 Artist Michael Browne once painted which famous United player as Jesus Christ?

46 Can you name either of the two famous English clubs Matt Busby played for?

47 Which player won caps with three different countries: Ukraine, Russia and the USSR/CIS?

48 Dennis Viollet holds the record for the most league goals scored by a United player in a season. Is his record 26, 29 or 32 goals?

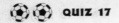
49 Which United manager, hearing of Salford Rugby Club's nickname, 'The Red Devils', declared that it should become United's nickname?

50 Which famous United player scored a record 41 FA Cup goals in the 1960s and 1970s?

 QUIZ 17

1 How many times did Manchester United play Leeds United in the 1991/92 season?

2 Which winger, nicknamed 'Merlin' by his team-mates, played on one wing whilst Steve Coppell played on the other wing?

3 In which season did United win the European Cup and finish second in the league: 1964/65, 1967/68 or 1971/72?

4 Was Lou Macari, Willie Morgan or Martin Buchan unsuccessfully sued for libel by the ex-United manager, Tommy Docherty?

5 Which player bagged 99 goals in just 145 games for Celtic before joining United for approximately £850,000?

6 In Alex Ferguson's first 1000 games in charge, did the team win: 346, 568 or 627 matches?

7 Did United beat Olympiakos, Brondby, Croatia Zagreb or Besiktas 5-0 and 6-2 in the 1998/99 Champions League?

8 Luke Chadwick, Danny Higginbotham and Ronnie Wallwork all played on loan for which Belgian club?

9 Which rivals of United's started life as Dial Square?

10 Which United forward had the nickname 'Sparky': Mark Hughes, Frank Stapleton or Peter Davenport?

11 Were Manchester United, Arsenal or Tottenham Hotspur the first team in the 20th century to win the League and FA Cup double?

12 Have Manchester United won the Charity Shield seven, fourteen or nineteen times?

13 Which former United youth team striker was at Watford and moved to Sheffield United for the 2005/06 season?

14 How many times have Manchester United won the UEFA Cup?

15 How many times have United won the Intercontinental Cup: once, twice or four times?

16 Did Bobby Charlton, Nobby Stiles or Denis Law win the European Footballer of the Year award in 1964?

17 United finished the 1980/81 season with seven wins in a row but which manager was sacked after the season?

18 Was Paul Ince transferred from United to Inter Milan, Parma or Lazio?

19 Which ex-United striker played the 2005/06 season for Villarreal?

20 From 1992/93 to the end of the 2004/05 season, which is the only side that United have a negative goal difference against in Premier League games?

21 In what year did the single *We All Follow Man United* reach number 10 in the charts?

22 Who scored the winning goal in the 1995/96 FA Cup Final to ensure Manchester United won a League and Cup double?

23 Sol Campbell was once a United youth team player: true or false?

24 How many games did United lose at home in the 2004/05 Premier League?

25 Which famous United attacker came on in the 91st minute in the 2005 FA Cup Final?

26 Who was made Life President of Manchester United in 1980?

27 George Best's final appearance for Manchester United was against Liverpool, Tottenham Hotspur or QPR?

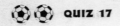

28 In 2005, what was the only stadium in Britain that held more spectators than Old Trafford?

29 To which Spanish club did United sell Mark Hughes?

30 Did Martin Buchan, Stuart Pearson or Jimmy Greenhoff score the winner in the 1977 FA Cup Final?

31 Which great attacking servant of the club cost only £1.5 million in 1996?

32 Former Manchester United player Norman Whiteside is now a podiatrist: true or false?

33 Old Trafford lies on a street named after a former manager. What is the street called?

34 Which United player's two transfers within the Premier League totalled around £48 million?

35 Who was the first United player to captain England at more than one World Cup?

36 In 1999, United recorded their biggest ever away win. Who did they beat 8-1?

37 How many years did it take to rebuild Old Trafford from its bombing in World War II?

38 Was Sir Matt Busby at United for 18, 24 or 32 years?

39 *Managing My Life* was a book about which Manchester United figure?

40 Can you name either of United's kit sponsor companies from the past whose names begin with the letter A?

41 For which club did Louis Saha play before joining United?

42 United were deducted a league point after a brawl in a 1990 game, against which team?

43 To which Premier League club did Phil Neville move from United?

44 Which two of the following players have played for both Manchester City and Manchester United: Gary Birtles, Dennis Tuert, Peter Barnes, Sammy McIlroy?

45 Which position does Sylvan Ebanks-Blake play: defence, midfield or attack?

46 Was Wayne Rooney's debut for United in the FA Cup, the Premier League or the Champions League?

47 From what country does eighteen-year-old striker, Dong Fangzhou, come?

48 At which Spanish ground did United win the Champions League?

49 Did Gary Walsh, Jordi Cruyff, Nick Culkin or Jonathon Greening's entire United first team career last 75 seconds, in August 1999?

50 At which stadium did United win the 1967/68 European Cup?

 QUIZ 18

1 United reached the semi-finals of the European Cup on their first three, four or five attempts?

2 Did it take Denis Law 139, 173 or 214 games to score his first 100 goals for United?

3 Which German club did Manchester United beat to win the Champions League?

4 Which United player was the only player to feature in all of England's 1998 World Cup qualifying games?

5 Which former United player became manager of Bradford City in the winter of 2003?

6 Before Eric Cantona, the last United player to win the Football Writers' Association Footballer of the Year was: Bryan Robson, Paul Ince or George Best?

7 Which former United centre back was the manager of Birmingham City at the start of the 2005/06 season?

8 Did Paddy Crerand, Alex Stepney or Steve Bruce play 401 games for United scoring fifteen times?

9   At the 1998 World Cup, which two French players, later to sign for United, would undergo a ritual before every game where one kissed the other's bald head?

10   Which ex-United striker, still playing in the Premier League, was playing for Millwall in 1985, the year Wayne Rooney was born?

11   United become the first team to win the League, FA Cup and Charity Shield in which season: 1967, 1991 or 1994?

12   Who scored Manchester United's first ever goal in the Premier League: Andy Cole, Steve Bruce, Mark Hughes or Roy Keane?

13   Against Bayer Leverkusen in November 2002, Manchester United were down to ten men, because: David Beckham got sent off; Roy Keane was sent off; or they got an injury after using all their substitutes?

14   How many months was Eric Cantona suspended for after his attack on a spectator in 1995?

15 Who cost United more to buy: Cristiano Ronaldo, Dwight Yorke or Andy Cole?

16 Which United player appeared on the first ever episode of the *A Question of Sport* TV quiz show in 1971?

17 Which striker joined Coventry City from Manchester United for £2 million in 1994?

18 What part of his body did Roy Keane break when playing against Liverpool in 2005?

19 Can you name one of the footballers who scored for United in 1995/96 whilst wearing the infamous grey shirts?

20 Who is United's longest-serving manager?

21 United reached the final of which competition in the same season that much of their team was wiped out in the Munich Air Disaster?

22 Whose last game in League football included scoring the goal that relegated Manchester United in 1974?

23 Was Eric Cantona, Andrei Kanchelskis or Mark Hughes United's leading goal scorer in the 1992/93 season?

24 What was the name of the sixteen-year-old groundsman who left the stands and went in goal for United during the 1956 Charity Shield game?

25 Which defender scored two goals as United played their two game qualifier for the 2005/06 Champions League and won 6-0 on aggregate?

26 Can you name either of the two teams Manchester United scored four goals against during their 2004/05 FA Cup campaign?

27 Against which team from the south coast of England did David Beckham make his first team debut?

28 Which striker scored a record seven hat-tricks in the 1963/64 season?

29 Which famous side did United beat at the semi-final stage 4-3 to get to the Final of the 1967/68 European Cup?

30 In the 2005/06 season, how many teams in the Premier League have names ending with the word 'United'?

31 Can you name two of the four clubs former Manchester United youth team winger, Keith Gillespie has played for?

32 Against which country did David Beckham captain England for the 50th time?

33 Giuseppe Rossi was signed by United from which Italian club: Lazio, Parma, Inter Milan or AC Milan?

34 The first game in Old Trafford in 1910 was against Liverpool, Royal Engineers or Bury?

35 Which United defender was sent off for headbutting Freddie Ljungberg in a 2005 game versus Arsenal?

36 Did United make a loss of £1.5 million, £3.5 million or £5 million on the sale of Kleberson?

37 Did Alex Stepney get one, three, five or nine caps for England?

38 Manchester United's purchase of Roy Carroll for £2 million remains the largest transfer fee received by which Premier League team?

39 Which United player retired at the top of his game aged just 26 yet went on to play for a variety of teams in Britain, America and Australia?

40 What was the name of the QPR goalkeeper United signed for a record £11,000 in 1950 who was a commando during World War II?

41 Is Harry Stafford, Frank Barson or Albert Quixall the only player to have captained Manchester United and their forerunners, Newton Heath?

42 How many million pounds did United sell Paul Ince for?

43 Which team has won the League Cup the fewest times out of Manchester United, Norwich City or Nottingham Forest?

44 Which famous United defender and captain broke his nose an astonishing six times during his career?

45 Manchester United never finished above Liverpool in the league during the 1970s: true or false?

46 *After the Ball* was a 2003 book about which United legend?

47 Manchester United played in the very first Charity Shield game. Were their opponents Arsenal, Bolton Wanderers, QPR or Liverpool?

48 In the 1990/91 season, did Manchester United or Manchester City finish in the higher position?

49 Was Jack Robson, Lal Hilditch or Walter Crickmer the only ever Manchester United player-manager?

50 Which player in the 2005/06 season has the Number 9 shirt?

HARD QUESTIONS

 QUIZ 1

1. Can you name the Yorkshire and England cricketer who played for United between 1972 and 1975?

2. Which former United manager was appointed as trainer of the English FA team for a 1970 tour of Australia?

3. In which Premier League season did United score a whopping 97 goals?

4. Can you name all four United players in the England squad for the 2002 World Cup finals?

5. Ice cream was allegedly the transfer fee when Hughie McLenahan moved from which club to Manchester United in 1927?

6. In *Best* – a film of George Best's life – which famous rock singer played the role of his friend, Rodney Marsh?

7 What was the nickname of the club, Newton Heath?

8 Which young defender spent four months at Royal Antwerp on loan and made his United debut in 2003 versus West Bromwich Albion in the Carling Cup?

9 United player Enoch West was banned by the Football Association in 1916. In which year was the ban lifted?

10 At which club's ground did Manchester United play St Etienne in the 1977/78 European Cup-Winners' Cup?

11 A club called Manchester United won the 1998/99 league championship – but in which country?

12 Who was the only ever Dutch player to play for his country in the years before and after he was at United but not whilst at the club?

13 Can you name either of the first two black players to play for England, both of whom went on to play for United?

14 What two colours were the shirts United changed into at half-time in their April 1996 game versus Southampton?

15 Which former manager of Manchester United died in the Munich Air Disaster in 1958?

16 Who was the first footballer Manchester United sold to another club for over a million pounds?

17 How many yellow cards did Bobby Charlton receive in his long career for England?

18 Which former Manchester United goalkeeper played cricket for Scotland against a full Australian Test team?

19 Can you name the three clubs in the same 2005/06 Champions League first round group as United?

20 Accrington Stanley played Manchester United how many times in league games?

21 Against which Midlands team were United 5-0 up in just 22 minutes in 1966?

22 In 1930-31, United recorded their lowest number of league wins. How many games did they win in the 42 they played?

23 Arsenal had let in only seven goals in seventeen games before playing United in November 1990. How many had they let in in total after that game?

24 Which player appeared in every numbered outfield team shirt, from 2 to 14, between 1984 and 1994?

25 Who was United's first ever substitute in 1965 although he was not used in that game?

26 What airline owned the aircraft on which many Manchester United players and officials perished in the Munich Air Disaster?

27 Which United player and European Cup Winner's father used to drive the No. 47 bus past the Old Trafford ground?

28 The old Stretford End and Stretford Paddock was used the last time in 1992 for which player's testimonial game?

29 Which United legend played an incredible eighteen seasons for the club before later coaching the Chicago Sting and becoming a European scout for Japan's J-League?

30 Who was playing for Manchester United in December 2002 but 2005 saw him playing for Bacup Borough in the North West Counties League?

31 In 1972, what novelty song did Manchester United record and release as a single?

32 What was the name of the bald French defender who debuted for United against QPR in December 1995?

33 Under what name had Ryan Giggs played for England Schoolboys?

34 In 1960, Manchester United recorded their biggest ever win over Chelsea. What was the score?

35 Starting in 1999, how many Premier League games in a row did United play without there being a goalless draw?

36 What was the name of the hoaxer who appeared in a Manchester United official team photo before a 2001 Champions League game?

37 Which Eastern European team had United secured a 3-3 draw with just prior to the Munich Air Disaster?

38 What was the name of Manchester United's first ever goalkeeper from the United States?

39 Which goalkeeper has the shortest Manchester United first team career of any player?

40 Who is the only World Footballer of the Year to have ever played in the Premier League for two of United's rivals?

41 Which legendary United player played with a toothpick in the corner of his mouth, which he said helped him concentrate?

42 At what medium wave frequency would you find Manchester United's own radio station broadcasting on matchdays?

43 Which player, later United captain, broke his nose, gave away a penalty and was booked, on his debut?

44 Whose tally of four career goals for United came once every 113.75 games?

45 Bobby Charlton retired from United in 1973. In which year had he joined the club?

46 When Phil Neville left the club, how many goals had he scored more than his brother?

47 Which former United youth teamer was Brian Kidd's first signing at Blackburn Rovers?

48 Dave Sexton replaced Tommy Docherty as manager at two other clubs besides United. Can you name them?

49 United were runners-up in which 1967/68 international competition?

50 Who replaced United in the 1999/2000 FA Cup third round draw?

1 What is Malcolm Glazer's middle name?

2 In what competition did United take part in the first ever penalty shoot-out?

3 Which United manager had previously managed Weymouth FC and Torquay United?

4 Which winger made just four appearances for United before joining rivals, Manchester City?

5 Who did United have to play over two games to qualify for the 2005/06 Champions League?

6 Which United player, currently on loan, was just thirteen years old when he played in a World Cup qualifier?

7 Sir Alex Ferguson's first game in charge was a 2-0 league loss against which side?

8 Which United player, still at the club in 2005/06, scored their fastest ever goal in 1995, timed at fifteen seconds?

9   Can you name the former United player who as a teenager broke cricket batting records set by England cricketer, Michael Atherton?

10 Which United player and England World Cup winner married Johnny Giles's sister?

11 Newton Heath were declared bankrupt in 1902 with debts of £2600, £31,500 or £73,000?

12 Which United manager once rode from Land's End to John O'Groats by bicycle?

13 Who scored nine penalties for United in the 1974/75 season?

14 Which United player captained his country for the first time in 1994?

15 Who won a Welsh Cup Winners' medal in 1894 and, amazingly, played in an FA Cup semi-final in 1924, thirty years later?

16 Which member of the United club during the 2005/06 season was co-owner of the Portuguese A1 Grand Prix team along with Luis Figo?

17 In the 1999 film, *Best*, about George Best's life, which former United player appears, acting as a European referee?

18 Which electronics company were United's main sponsors from 1982 to 2000?

19 Name all three United players who went with Scotland to the 1974 World Cup?

20 Which two of the following United players wore contact lenses: Brian Greenhoff, Lee Sharpe, Jordi Cruyff, Nobby Stiles?

21 Which United midfielder played over 70 minutes of the 1976 FA Cup Final with a broken toe?

22 Who were United playing in 1974 when referee, Clive Thomas took both teams off for five minutes to calm them down?

23 Which United player had the nickname 'Dolly'?

24 How old was Steve Coppell when he became the football league's youngest manager of the time?

25 Which United goalkeeper dislocated his jaw whilst shouting at his team-mates?

26 Which United full back's other clubs included Chester City, West Bromwich Albion, Dundee and Norwegian side, Molde?

27 What was the name of the 1994 Manchester United song which reached number one in the charts?

28 Which United player was promised a public house as a reward if he captained United back into the First Division, and got his wish in 1925?

29 Who managed to score on his debut in five different cup competitions for United?

30 In 1995, United's Keith Kent was awarded the Premier League's: Supporter, Groundsman or Physiotherapist of the Year?

31 Who were England's opponents in 1926 on the very first England match played at Old Trafford?

32 When England played South Africa in
    1997 at Old Trafford, how many years
    was it since the last England football
    match at the ground?

33 Apart from Bobby Charlton and Nobby
    Stiles, who was the third United player in
    England's 1966 World Cup squad?

34 Who was chairman of Manchester United
    between 1951 to 1965?

35 In 1989, which Scottish club did United
    play in a friendly to raise money for the
    Lockerbie air disaster?

36 Which ex-United captain shares the same
    birthday as Sir Alex Ferguson?

37 What was the only final of a European
    competition that United played in wearing
    white shirts?

38 How many players whose surname begins
    with the letter S played for Manchester
    United in the 1998/99 Champions
    League Final?

39   In 1977 United were forced to play a European Cup-Winners' Cup game at the ground furthest from them in England. What was the name of the ground?

40   Who scored the only goal to give United victory in the World Club Championship Final in November 1999?

41   Which United father and son were the first father and son to each win a league championship with the same club?

42   Who did United beat 5-0 in their last game at the Bank Street ground before moving to Old Trafford?

43   Which former United striker was the club's oldest scorer of a hat-trick after scoring three goals in a 2000 game?

44   Which England cricket captain's brother played for Brighton against United in the 1983 FA Cup Final?

45   How many of the starting eleven who won the European Cup in 1968 had Sir Matt Busby spent money on transfers to bring in?

46 Who was the only team United beat away in the league during the whole of the 1986/87 season?

47 What was the name of the league United were in between 1940 and 1946?

48 George Best played against Manchester United reserves in an August 1973 game which his side won 3-2. Which team was he playing for?

49 Which United player made his debut for England in the same game that saw Bobby Charlton win his 100th cap?

50 Harald Halse appeared in FA Cup Finals for Manchester United and two other clubs. Can you name either of them?

ANSWERS

Easy Quiz

1. Old Trafford
2. Red
3. Chelsea
4. Goalkeeper
5. Sir Alex Ferguson
6. Midfield
7. Sunderland
8. 2005
9. True
10. 'The Red Devils'

11. Chelsea
12. Eric Cantona
13. 1998/99
14. Jaap Stam
15. Wayne Rooney
16. The Netherlands
17. Gary and Phil Neville
18. Arsenal
19. True
20. Roy Keane

21. Italy
22. Manchester United
23. Liverpool
24. United

25. Republic of Ireland
26. Sir Alex Ferguson
27. France
28. Manchester United
29. Arsenal
30. Jimmy

31. The 1950s
32. Black
33. Once
34. False
35. Germany
36. American
37. Norway
38. Liverpool
39. True
40. Gary Neville

41. Celtic
42. White
43. Quinton Fortune
44. Manchester United
45. Bobby Charlton
46. Fulham
47. Rio Ferdinand
48. Phil Neville
49. France
50. Manchester United 5,
    Burton Albion 0

Quiz 1

1. Steve Bruce
2. Gary Pallister
3. The Charity Shield
4. Arnold Muhren
5. Denis Law
6. Eric Cantona
7. Denis Irwin
8. Ryan Giggs

9. Chris Eagles
10. False

11. One
12. A goalkeeper
13. Everton's
14. Kleberson
15. Jaap Stam
16. White shirts
17. *Manchester United Ruined My Life*

18. Aston Villa, Newcastle United
19. Gordon Strachan
20. Four

21. Gaelic Football
22. Tommy Docherty
23. Wayne Rooney
24. Brian McClair
25. Ryan Giggs
26. West Ham United
27. Roger Byrne
28. Tommy Taylor
29. Teddy Sheringham
30. 1958/59

31. £60,000
32. George Best
33. Monaco
34. Dave Sexton
35. Henning Berg
36. Ryan Giggs
37. Munich
38. Paul Scholes
39. Lee Martin
40. £800,000

41. Barthez
42. 11
43. Third
44. Paul Scholes
45. Walsall
46. Patrick Viera
47. Sheffield Wednesday
48. Aston Villa
49. West Ham United
50. Poland

Quiz 2

1. Roy Keane
2. Chelsea
3. Nike
4. 1956
5. Rupert Murdoch
6. Theatre of Dreams
7. France
8. Mikael Silvestre

9. Four
10. The 1960s

11. Sir Matt Busby
12. Denis Law
13. Bryan Robson
14. Mark Hughes (two goals)
15. Peter Schmeichel
16. The architect of Old Trafford
17. Arsenal
18. Barnet
19. Win
20. Sheffield United
    (player/manager)

21. Maccabi Haifa
22. Juan Sebastian Veron
23. 1993/94
24. Gary Pallister
25. Monaco
26. George Best
27. Hartlepool United, Carlisle
    United, Newcastle United
28. Middlesbrough
29. Raimond van der Gouw
30. Rapid Vienna

31. Vasco da Gama, Nexaca
32. Frank Stapleton
33. George Best
34. Alex Stepney
35. Mickey Thomas
36. False
37. George Best
38. Fenerbahce
39. Sir Matt Busby
40. Ronaldo

41. Portugal
42. Aston Villa
43. Newton Heath
44. Ajax
45. Rio Ferdinand
46. Joe Spence
47. Bobby Charlton
48. Ray Wilkins
49. Gary Birtles
50. Fred The Red

Quiz 3

1. Darren Fletcher
2. Spartak Moscow
3. Stuart Pearson
4. The European Champions Cup
5. The Netherlands
6. George Best
7. One
8. Manchester United
9. Jordi Cruyff
10. Dave Sexton

11. Chelsea
12. Ruud van Nistelrooy
13. Jimmy Hill
14. Fenerbahce
15. 1956/57
16. Everton
17. Kieran Richardson
18. Number 13
19. Four
20. Crystal Palace

21. Yes, two.
22. Newcastle United
23. Ole Gunnar Solskjaer
24. 394
25. Newcastle United
26. Brad Friedel
27. Wales
28. Preston North End
    (he was out on loan).
29. Railway workers
30. 2003

31. Manchester United
32. First
33. Three
34. Shay Brennan
35. Five
36. Dion Dublin
37. Tim Howard
38. Six
39. Gary Walsh
40. 200th goal

41. Paul Ince
42. Rangers

43. Charlie Roberts
44. Ole Gunnar Solskjaer
45. Republic of Ireland
46. Millwall
47. Denis Law
48. Blackburn Rovers
49. Ryan Giggs
50. Sean Connery

Quiz 4

1. Charlton Athletic
2. Wes Brown
3. David McCreery
4. Chris Eagles
5. Fabien Barthez
6. Ruud van Nistelrooy
7. Wayne Rooney
8. Arsenal
9. Peter Schmeichel
10. Wayne Rooney

11. *United*
12. Five
13. Brazil
14. Eleven
15. Dwight Yorke
16. Bryan Robson
17. Kleberson
18. Leeds United
19. Dwight Yorke
20. Kleberson

21. Bobby Charlton
22. 10-1
23. Paul Ince
24. Bolton Wanderers
25. Ray Wilkins
26. Watford
27. 2003
28. Yes
29. Mexico
30. Cristiano Ronaldo

31. Roy Keane
32. The FA Cup
33. Coolmore
34. Lee Sharpe
35. Sergeant Major

36. Kevin Moran
37. Ryan Giggs
38. Johnny Carey
39. A goalkeeper
40. Dixie Dean

41. Wimbledon
42. Six
43. Alan Smith
44. Cristiano Ronaldo
    (after Ronald Reagan)
45. Andy Cole
46. Leeds United
47. Duncan Edwards
48. Carrington
49. Debrecen
50. Ruud van Nistelrooy

Quiz 5

1. FC United of Manchester
2. Sunderland
3. Fourth
4. Alan Gowling
5. Paul Scholes, Ruud van
   Nistelrooy, Ryan Giggs,
   Ole Gunnar Solskjaer
6. Gary Bailey
7. Alan Curbishley
8. Southampton
9. Portsmouth
10. Birmingham City

11. Palmeiras
12. Huddersfield, Manchester City,
    Everton
13. 30 goals
14. South Melbourne
15. Brian
16. FA Cup
17. Denis Law
18. The FA Cup Final
19. First: George Best,
    Second: Bobby Charlton
20. Paul Scholes

21. Ole Gunnar Solskjaer
22. Norman Whiteside
23. David Beckham's

24. Gary Neville
25. Hibs
26. Cristiano Ronaldo
27. Alan Smith
28. Gary Bailey
29. The Cliff
30. Sparta Prague

31. Bobby Charlton
32. Ron Atkinson
33. Benfica
34. Andy Cole
35. Four times
36. Spain
37. Shamrock Rovers
38. Fulham
39. 2003
40. Manchester City

41. Mark Hughes
42. Inter Milan
43. A mobile phone company
44. Graeme Souness
45. Number 5
46. Denis Law
47. Celtic
48. Mike Phelan
49. Tommy Docherty
50. Third

Quiz 6

1. Charlton Athletic
2. 59
3. Bryan Robson
4. Cricket
5. Roy Keane
6. Blue
7. Duncan Edwards
8. South Africa
9. George Best
10. 2002

11. Eighteen games
12. Arsenal
13. Ron Atkinson
14. Manchester United
15. Steve Bruce
16. Manchester City

17. Blackburn Rovers
18. Newcastle United
19. Ten points
20. True

21. Norwich City
22. Bobby Charlton
23. 82 goals
24. Bari, Verona, Lazio and Fiorentina
25. Chapman
26. Dennis Walker
27. Paul McGrath
28. All four
29. Fulham
30. Greece

31. Three
32. Denis Law
33. The semi-final
34. Won (1-0)
35. Bryan Robson
36. Bobby Charlton
37. Bolton Wanderers
38. Gainsborough Trinity
39. 2002 World Cup
40. Sheffield Wednesday, Aston Villa

41. Danny Wallace
42. Eric Cantona
43. Brian and Jimmy Greenhoff
44. Floodlights
45. QPR
46. Southampton
47. A penalty
48. Frank O'Farrell
49. Bryan Robson
50. Lou Macari

Quiz 7

1. 2003 League Cup
2. Ruud van Nistelrooy
3. Paul Scholes
4. Robert Pires
5. Harry Gregg, Bill Foulkes
6. Newcastle United
7. Neil Webb

8. Republic of Ireland
9. Two – Wayne Rooney and Rio Ferdinand
10. Bryan Robson

11. Chelsea
12. Diego Forlan
13. Mark Hughes
14. Nottingham Forest
15. Wimbledon (now MK Dons)
16. Wayne Rooney
17. 1967/68
18. Charlton Athletic
19. Fifteen times
20. Arsenal

21. Eric Cantona
22. Left back
23. Johnny Carey
24. Colin Heath, Tom Heaton
25. Andy Cole
26. Ryan Giggs
27. Leslie
28. Number 8
29. His knee
30. Gary Bailey

31. Newcastle United, Exeter City (in the FA Cup)
32. False
33. Norway
34. Crystal Palace
35. Sir Matt Busby
36. Tommy Taylor
37. Roy Carroll
38. Crystal Palace
39. Bobby Charlton
40. 24 games

41. Tim Howard's
42. 1980
43. Bryan Robson
44. Portsmouth
45. Two
46. Brian McClair
47. Yes
48. None
49. Massimo Taibi
50. Ruud van Nistelrooy

Quiz 8

1. Eric Cantona
2. Both
3. Millwall
4. Ronny Johnsen
5. Burton Albion
6. Ruud van Nistelrooy
7. Yugoslavia
8. Celtic
9. José Mourinho
10. 56 games

11. England
12. Leeds United
13. Stoke City
14. George Graham
15. One
16. Alex Stepney
17. Barnsley
18. North Road
19. 32 goals
20. Manchester United,
    Tottenham Hotspur,
    Portsmouth and
    West Ham United

21. Wrexham, Sparta Rotterdam,
    Wolverhampton Wanderers
22. Bryan Robson
23. 11%
24. Bryan Robson
25. Eric Djemba-Djemba
26. Joel, Avram and Bryan
27. Bottom
28. None
29. Scottish
30. Dennis Viollet

31. 2001
32. Paul Ince
33. Wales
34. The FA Cup
35. 1993
36. The North Stand
37. Paul Parker
38. Bobby Charlton
39. West Bromwich Albion
40. Blackburn Rovers

41. USA
42. Henning Berg
43. Wayne Rooney
44. True
45. His tonsils
46. Brian Kidd
47. Sir Matt Busby
48. Wayne Rooney
49. Garth Crooks
50. Manchester City

Quiz 9

1. Eight
2. 2004
3. Mike Duxbury
4. Sir Matt Busby
5. Greg Dyke
6. Ole Gunnar Solskjaer
7. Bahrain
8. Ole Gunnar Solskjaer
9. Fourteen goals
10. 40

11. Eighteen points
12. Manchester City
13. The Netherlands
14. More than eight
15. 1784 goals
16. Gordon Hill
17. Ron Atkinson
18. Fourteen goals
19. True
20. Bobby and Jack Charlton

21. Bryan Robson
22. Brian Kerr
23. Sammy McIlroy
24. Frank Stapleton
25. European Super Cup and
    Inter-Continental Cup
26. £10.3 million
27. Tommy Docherty
28. Charlton Athletic,
    Wigan Athletic
29. Gary and Phil Neville
30. Eric Cantona

31. Stuart Pearson

32. Gary Pallister
33. Sir Matt Busby
34. Carlisle United
35. Billy Meredith, John Gidman
36. Oakwell
37. 2002
38. Kieran Richardson
39. Each goal was scored against a different goalkeeper
40. Bobby and Jack Charlton

41. Win
42. West Bromwich Albion
43. Gordon Strachan
44. David Beckham
45. Two million pounds
46. Three
47. West Bromwich Albion
48. Bill Foulkes
49. The Charity Shield
50. 1998 (1997/98 season)

Quiz 10

1. Real Madrid
2. Denis Law
3. Preston North End
4. True
5. The FA Cup
6. Score a penalty against Manchester United
7. Ron Greenwood
8. George Best
9. Laurent Blanc
10. Blackburn Rovers

11. Alan Gowling
12. Paul Scholes
13. One point
14. Tampa Bay Buccaneers

15. 1996
16. Barcelona
17. George Best
18. Bryan Robson
19. The European Super Cup
20. Inter Milan

21. Karel Poborsky

22. Andy Cole
23. David Herd
24. Denis Law
25. Queens Park Rangers (QPR)
26. Three (Rooney, Ronaldo and van Nistelrooy)
27. 190
28. Mathematics
29. Everton
30. Nobby Stiles

31. South Korea
32. Chelsea (1988)
33. 1993
34. Highbury
35. Colombia
36. Argentina
37. Megastore
38. Blackpool
39. Tommy Docherty
40. Mick McCarthy

41. Ryan Giggs
42. George Best
43. Mark Hughes
44. Two (Sir Matt Busby and Walter Crickmer)
45. Cameroon
46. Ruud van Nistelrooy
47. Nobby Stiles
48. Seventeen
49. Denis Law
50. Brighton

Quiz 11

1. Peter Schmeichel
2. Never
3. Parma
4. Norman Whiteside, George Best
5. 94
6. Chelsea
7. Nobby Stiles
8. John O'Shea
9. Gary Bailey
10. Benfica
11. Aston Villa

12. Stan Pearson (149 goals)
13. Alan Hansen
14. Rio Ferdinand
15. Two
16. West Ham United
17. Wales
18. Ruud van Nistelrooy
19. Middlesbrough
20. Wayne Rooney

21. Uruguay
22. £171.5 million
23. Lou Macari
24. 1992
25. BSkyB
26. Sir Matt Busby Way
27. Vodafone
28. Steve McClaren
29. Bryan Robson
30. Newcastle United

31. Henning Berg
32. Bolton Wanderers
33. 90 caps
34. Everton
35. Martin Buchan
36. Alan Shearer
37. Peter Schmeichel
38. £22,000
39. Red Star Belgrade
40. Third

41. Charlton Athletic, Everton
42. Sir Alex Ferguson
43. Everton
44. Nicky Butt
45. The Coronation Cup
46. Ron Atkinson
47. 1998
48. Newcastle United
49. Karel Poborsky
50. Second division

Quiz 12

1. Ernest Mangall
2. Neil Webb
3. George Best
4. Kaspar Schmeichel

5. Mikael Silvestre
6. Ray Wilkins, Bryan Robson
7. Wigan Athletic
8. Oldham Athletic, Leeds United
9. Denis Law
10. Third-most

11. Ole Gunnar Solskjaer
12. Manchester United
13. Portugal
14. Everton
15. One
16. False
17. Charlton Athletic
18. Les Sealey
19. 1998 World Cup
20. Brian Kidd

21. Paul Scholes
22. Giuseppe Rossi
23. Gary Pallister
24. Charlton Athletic
25. Ryan Giggs
26. Sir Bobby Robson
27. Norman Whiteside
28. Bobby Charlton
29. 1941
30. Third

31. Aberdeen
32. Les Sealey
33. Eric Cantona
34. Bolton Wanderers
35. Manchester City and Aston Villa
36. Wigan Athletic
37. March
38. Arsenal
39. Ajax
40. Ruud van Nistelrooy

41. West Ham United
42. Manchester City
43. Chelsea
44. 2004
45. Tommy Docherty
46. Luton Town
47. Southampton
48. £10,000

49. 23
50. Louis Saha

Quiz 13

1. Everton, Southampton, Manchester City
2. 1996
3. Porto
4. 1997
5. England
6. Denis Irwin
7. Anderlecht
8. Denis Law
9. Hadjuk Split
10. Wendy Toms

11. The 1920s and the 1930s
12. Ruud van Nistelrooy
13. Barcelona
14. The Red Café
15. Swindon Town
16. Chas Richards
17. Grey
18. Leeds United
19. Twice
20. £18 million

21. Four
22. Ten
23. Liverpool
24. Number 7
25. One
26. Four
27. Frank O'Farrell
28. True
29. 1941
30. Chelsea

31. Darren Fletcher
32. Dwight Yorke, Andy Cole
33. Dwight Yorke
34. Aston Villa
35. Roy Keane
36. Brian Kidd
37. Lee Sharpe
38. Benfica
39. Danny Wallace
40. More than 400

41. Juventus
42. Three
43. Rugby Union
44. Cristiano Ronaldo
45. Ruud van Nistelrooy
46. 1992
47. None
48. David Beckham
49. Pat Jennings
50. American

Quiz 14

1. Peter Davenport
2. Chelsea
3. Australia
4. Swindon Town
5. 1989
6. September 2003
7. Ipswich
8. Sporting Lisbon
9. 1980
10. Juventus

11. Reg Allen, Harry Gregg, Alex Stepney, Fabien Barthez,
12. Rock of Gibraltar
13. Jaap Stam
14. Preston North End
15. Ruud Van Nistelrooy
16. Gabriel Heinze
17. Brian Kidd, Denis Law
18. Real Madrid
19. Aberdeen
20. One

21. 1958
22. Mark Hughes
23. Tottenham Hotspur
24. The West Stand
25. Six goals
26. Jesper Olsen, Johnny Sivebaek
27. Over 1000 points
28. Ruud van Nistelrooy
29. Eric Cantona
30. 1973/74

31. 1992
32. 13 (13-1)

33. Crewe Alexandra
34. Neville
35. Barnsley
36. Paul Ince
37. Brian Kidd
38. George Best
39. Nottingham Forest
40. Leeds United

41. AC Milan
42. Harry Gregg
43. The Czech Republic
44. 61 consecutive games
45. David Beckham
46. Martin Edwards
47. Semi-final stage
48. Fenerbahce
49. Gary Neville
50. Ryan Giggs

Quiz 15

1. Bill Foulkes
2. Five
3. Cristiano Ronaldo
4. Full back
5. Four
6. Gordon Strachan
7. Eight
8. Luke Chadwick
9. Dennis Bergkamp
10. Eleven penalties

11. City 4 United 1
12. St Mirren
13. Charlton Athletic
14. 2000/01
15. The European Cup-Winners' Cup
16. José Antonio Reyes
17. Jesper Olsen
18. George Best
19. Paul Scholes
20. 1908

21. Andrei Kanchelskis
22. Hong Kong
23. Manchester United, Blackpool, Newcastle

24. Tottenham Hotspur
25. Cristiano Ronaldo
26. Twelve years
27. David May
28. Denis Irwin, Paul Ince
29. Ipswich Town
30. Jack Rowley

31. AC Milan
32. Quinton Fortune
33. AC Milan
34. PSV Eindhoven
35. Herbert Bamlett
36. Suggesting it changed its name to Manchester United
37. Kevin Moran
38. Dennis Irwin
39. UNICEF
40. November

41. False
42. Steve Coppell
43. None
44. Michael Owen
45. Brian McClair
46. Denis Law
47. Bury
48. Blackburn Rovers
49. Tottenham Hotspur
50. Ernest Mangall

Quiz 16

1. True
2. Chelsea
3. Lou Macari
4. Hungary
5. 92
6. Eric Cantona
7. South Stand
8. Ryan Giggs
9. Ruud van Nistelrooy
10. Preston North End

11. Roy Keane
12. Mark Bosnich
13. Walter Winterbottom
14. Aberdeen
15. 1999

16. Tommy Taylor
17. Coventry City
18. Grey
19. Manchester United
20. Argentina

21. Tim Howard
22. Blacksmith
23. Mario Basler
24. Hampden Park, White Hart Lane
25. Kieran Richardson
26. One
27. Scotland
28. Mark Bosnich
29. 1957
30. £50

31. Denis Law
32. Roy Keane
33. Elton John
34. Newcastle United
35. 1999/2000
36. Andrei Kanchelskis
37. 0-0
38. Baxter
39. £450
40. Carlos Queiroz

41. Old Trafford
42. Frank O'Farrell
43. Liverpool
44. Andrei Kanchelskis
45. Eric Cantona
46. Liverpool, Manchester City
47. Andrei Kanchelskis
48. 32 goals
49. Matt Busby
50. Denis Law

Quiz 17

1. Four
2. Gordon Hill
3. 1967/68
4. Willie Morgan
5. Brian McClair
6. 568

7. Brondby
8. Royal Antwerp
9. Arsenal
10. Mark Hughes

11. Tottenham Hotspur
12. Fourteen times
13. Danny Webber
14. None
15. Once
16. Denis Law
17. Dave Sexton
18. Inter Milan
19. Diego Forlan
20. Chelsea

21. 1985
22. Eric Cantona
23. False
24. One
25. Ryan Giggs
26. Sir Matt Busby
27. QPR
28. Millennium Stadium, Cardiff
29. Barcelona
30. Jimmy Greenhoff

31. Ole Gunnar Solskjaer
32. True
33. Sir Matt Busby Way
34. Rio Ferdinand
35. Bryan Robson
36. Nottingham Forest
37. Eight
38. 24 years
39. Sir Alex Ferguson
40. Admiral and Adidas

41. Fulham
42. Arsenal
43. Everton
44. Peter Barnes, Sammy McIlroy
45. Attack
46. The Champions League
47. China
48. The Nou Camp
49. Nick Culkin
50. Wembley Stadium